PARANORMAL
FOREST OF DEAN

PARANORMAL
FOREST OF DEAN

ROSS ANDREWS

AMBERLEY

First published 2010

Amberley Publishing Plc
Cirencester Road, Chalford,
Stroud, Gloucestershire, GL6 8PE

www.amberley-books.com

British Library Cataloguing in Publication Data.
A catalogue record for this book is available from the British Library.

ISBN 978 1 84868 591 8

Typesetting and Origination by FONTHILLDESIGN.
Printed in the UK.

CONTENTS

Introduction   7
About the Author   9
A Brief History of The Forest of Dean   11

Chapter 1   Royal Forest Route Part One   13
             St. Briavel's Castle (part one), St. Briavel's – The George Inn,
             Brockhollands, Sling – The Miners Arms, Clearwell Caves,
             Clearwell Castle, Puzzlewood, Perrygrove Railway,
             Coleford – Angel Hotel, Coleford Police Station, Coleford – The Coombs

Chapter 2   Royal Forest Route Part Two   33
             Parkend – The Fountain Inn, Parkend – The Woodman Inn,
             Speech house, Beechenhurst and Nags Head Nature Reserve (big cats),
             Hopewell colliery

Chapter 3   Littledean   53
             Littledean Hall, The Bridge, Littledean House Hotel,
             Littledean Jail – The Crime Through Time Museum

Chapter 4   Other Forest Venues   59
             Goodrich Castle, Tintern Abbey, Raglan Castle

Chapter 5   St. Briavel's Castle   61
             The history, Phantomfest,
             The Main Castle – Lower floors, *The Castles Dog, The Peeping Ghost,*
             The Footsteps on the Stairs, The Ladies' Loo, The Horses,
             The Banging Noises, Slamming Door.
             The Main Castle – Upper floors, *The Crying Baby, The Floating Lights,*
             Smoke, Light, and Ink, Footsteps, Red Roger, Moving Chairs,
             Ouija Boards, The Woman In White, The Violins, The Young Girl,
             The Arguments and the Fights, Lights in the State Apartments,
             The Knocking, The Phantom Pillow, Electrical Interference.
             The East Tower – *The Chaplains Room, Footsteps, Another Dark Figure,*

CONTENTS

Children, Flashes of Light, The Neck Toucher, The Rich Ghost,
The Bed Hopping Ghost, The Curtain Twitcher.
The Constables Room *– The BOL, Flapping Doors,*
Physical Personal Attacks.
The Oubliette *– The Scary Bed, Temperatures Going Wild, BOLS,*
The Touchy Feely Ghostie, Conversations, Rattling Chains and Padlocks,
Mary, Recordings, The Black Shadow, Under the Door.
The West Tower *– **The Hanging Room, and Guard Room,***
The Figure in the Doorway, Floating Lights, BOLS and Mist,
The Tap on the Window, Foreign Witnesses, Marbles, Footsteps,
Grabbing Ghost, Messy Spirits, EMF Results, The Bed Hopper
Strikes Again, The Heavy Breather, Scrying, Get Off My Chair, Very Funny.
The Prison and the Room Outside *– Misty Figures,*
Another Grabbing Ghost, The Growling Ghost, A Ghostly Breeze,
BOLS, Knock Knock Who's There?, Footsteps.
The Old Kitchen *– Tom the Poltergeist, A Fidgeting Ghost,*
The Ghostly Hand, More People Than There Should Be, Not Really A Ghost.
The Porters Lodge *– The Always Opening Doors, Hagging,*
More Rolling Coins, The Crying Baby.
The Grounds and the Car Park *– The Knight, Knock Knock Who's*
There? Part Two, Footsteps, Something In The Trees, The Floating Legs,
Disappearing People, More Falling Stones, Undead Parking Attendant,
A Word Of Warning.

Chapter 6   More Information on How to be a Ghost Hunter   119
              Scrying, Psychometry, Psi Wheels, Calling Out, Weather Watching,
              Example of Report Forms, Zenner Experiments, Photography
              Orbs Problems, Computer Software.

Conclusions and Further Reading   125

INTRODUCTION

For those of you who know me, 'Hello again', hopefully you read my first book on ghost hunting, *Paranormal Cheltenham*, and you have ventured into the book shop to buy a second outstanding outing of spookiness from myself. If you have not read the first book then consider that last sentence a shameless advertisement. My previous book took in a reasonably small area, that being Cheltenham and Prestbury (allegedly the most haunted place in the UK).

This book has set its net a little wider, taking in the area of the Forest of Dean, mostly known as The Royal Forest Route. The Forest area can range from as far south as Chepstow up to Gloucester, and across to Ross on Wye. We are going to focus on the area right in the centre of the Forest, and maybe in the second book we can branch out through the Forest and take in Chepstow, Monmouth, and Ross on Wye, because I have so many stories there are easily two or three books of forest ghosts.

This Cheptsow, Gloucester, and Ross on Wye vicinity makes a Bermuda Triangle style area of ghostliness, a geometric haunted area, and also one of outstanding beauty. We will hear tales of ghosts and ghouls from Coleford, Clearwell, and Littledean, and the most haunted building I have ever investigated, which is St. Briavel's castle. Not only am I going to tell you of the strange other worldly entities that roam the Forest, and by that I am not having a sly dig at the lovely people who live there, but instead I am talking of the weird animals. There are now wild boars roaming around the Forest, but more importantly, be on the lookout for big cats. I myself have seen one, and not far from here there has been at least one person attacked by a panther roaming the forest.

In the last book I took you on ghost walks around Cheltenham, but I think it would be cruel of me to send you on walks around the Forest. It is a truly beautiful area of the world, and you could do a lot worse than spending the entire year walking around it looking at the flora and fauna. However, I realise that some of you might not want a 20 mile hike around haunted venues, so I will group them together so if you are on holiday you can pick and choose where to go for your fix of spookiness. I will even tell you where you can stay really cheaply in youth hostels, which are not only cheap but also haunted.

The best thing about ghost hunting is that strange feeling you get, the feeling that is similar to getting on a ghost train or roller coaster at the fair, or Alton Towers. We all for some reason like being spooked, because when we have calmed down we get relaxed and feel more secure about ourselves and our surroundings. That adrenaline rush is the best narcotic you can have, but I warn you it is very addictive. Once you tread into the shoes of a ghost hunter you will never go back. I have taken many a friend on a ghost hunt; they thought it would be a little bit of fun, an evening out to tell everyone about back at work on Monday. These people now regularly come ghost hunting with me, spending small fortunes on night vision cameras, EMF meters, heat sensitive video units, and as many things they can find on eBay as possible. Now speaking of EMF meters I will explain what these do later, but to put it quickly they are Electro Magnetic Frequency detectors, and not the band of the same name that happen to come from within the Forest itself.

I decided it would be a very good idea in this book to try and concentrate on places that you can actually go into, such as haunted caves and mines, castles you can stay in, museums to look around, and there are even gloriously beautiful walks through the woodland. I suggest you visit these areas in the daytime though, as the Forest is a scary place in the dark especially if you don't know whether it is a ghost following you, or an escaped panther or wild boar.

If you read the last book you will see a section on How to Be a Ghost Hunter, and at the end of this book I will try and add a few things to this to keep you going on your path of investigations. Do not worry if you have not read the first book, I will keep it nice and simple for the novice apprentice spook hunter to join in with.

The Graveyard at St. Briavel's Church.

ABOUT THE AUTHOR

So who am I? I have a history in Paranormal research as I am the Chairman of the Cheltenham-based Paranormal Society known as PARASOC, and have been for many years now. I have investigated and experienced paranormal phenomena throughout my whole life, and yet I am still a sceptical investigator.

Don't panic. I will not reprint the chapter from the previous book, or go on for too long as I am sure you would rather start looking for ghosts than look at my life history. The one thing to note as I have already said is that I am actually a sceptical ghost investigator, I have seen many a ghost and many a strange occurrence has gone on near and around me. That does not mean that I believe in afterlives, life after death, fairies, trolls, gnomes, bogeymen, and various other things that would make me in your eyes a NUTTER!

It is perfectly fine to say I believe in ghosts without fear that everyone is going to brand me as a witch and chase me out of town to huge howls of derision and laughter. I have mentioned in previous publications that you will rarely find an adult in this country that has not had some brush with the paranormal world. Even if you have not seen a ghost yourself I bet you know a story about your friend who saw a hooded figure in their upstairs lavatory, or a strange dark figure that emanated from the corner of the room.

I have spent many years investigating these very phenomena, and will hopefully spend many more. In my work as a paranormal scientist I have come across far scarier people than I have ever been scared by spooks. I have met many a fraudulent medium, but I am open minded enough to not discredit every medium, and tar them all with the same brush. I have met hundreds of very misguided ghost hunters who think every noise and light is a ghost, and not a radiator clicking and a car headlight. I have seen many people fall foul of psychic conmen and women who are only there to relieve you of your well earned cash. I have seen companies charge extortionate amounts of money for pieces of useless equipment for ghost hunting, and other companies charge small fortunes to stay in a supposedly haunted house with a medium that not only knows all the ghost stories attached to the building, but also knows the names and addresses of everyone present, so it is not too hard to Google information about them.

I mention all these things not to discredit any other parapsychologist but more to point out that I am not a strange eccentric who cannot grasp reality, and I do not only live in a supernatural world of my own creating. Instead I am a rationalist, and I would class myself as the best type of ghost hunter: one that keeps an open mind, for remember that a truly sceptical person is just as fanatic as a true over-the-top believer in everything.

A photo of me looking scarier than the actual ghosts.

Carrie's (aged 8 and a half) interpretation of me meeting a ghost.

A BRIEF HISTORY OF THE FOREST OF DEAN

I do not wish us to get too bogged down in the history of the Forest as this is primarily a ghost book, but I do think it is important to tell you a few words so that you can place in your mind a framework of where these ghosts may have originated from.

The Forest of Dean's name really refers to an area which has its boundaries marked by the river Severn, and the river Wye. Although its name is of doubtful origin we do know that the Saxons had a word called 'Dene' and this referred to a dale, or den. It may be from the 'Danes' who seemed to settle here for a while. It may also come from the word 'Arden' a Gaul and Briton word meaning woodland.

These Saxons were not the first to settle here. We have many records of habitation going back thousands of years, and the Druids seemed to use the rocks here for sacrificial purposes. The 'Buck Stone' is a huge rock on the crest of Staunton Hill, used for just this purpose.

The ancients were replaced by a not so relatively ancient people: the Romans. The reason they loved the forest so much was because of the natural abundance of Iron Ore. They built many mines here known as 'Scowles', and many Roman artefacts have been found in the forest vicinity. This continues to this day, but one report from back in 1780 by Mr. Wyrall tells us of a few artefacts:

"Coins, fibula, and other things known to be in use with that people, have been frequently found in the beds of cinders at certain places: this has occurred particularly at the village of Whitchurch."

He makes a note of one coin of 'Trajan', it struck him more than the others as it looked particularly fresh and perfect, especially when you consider how long it had lain there in the ground. He also recalls an instance of seeing a little image of brass, about four inches long, of a very elegant female figure, in a dancing pose.

This is not all of the discoveries. Numerous other items have been found including a Roman pavement, bricks, and tiles at Whitchurch; a camp, bath, and tessellated pavement at Lydney; and various coins from the reign of various rulers, including the emperor Claudius, have been found on the Coppet Woodhill, at Lydbrook, Perry Grove, and Crabtree Hill. So just from this small snippet of history we can see there has been a great amount of people milling around the area for a long period of time, always very conducive to ghost tales.

The Romans left their scars in the landscape but we can jump forward a few hundred years and see even more. Around the year 760 we had King Offa building a large dyke to separate the Welsh from the English, and there are various earthworks throughout this area that may be indications of the southernmost part of these fortifications

We can also jump forward to the reign of Henry II in the year A.D.1140 when the abbey of Flaxley was founded by Roger, Earl of Hereford's eldest son who named it, "The Abbey of St. Mary de Dene". Not long after King John has his favourite hunting lodge in the forest in the form of St. Briavel's Castle, this in my experience has to be the most haunted building in the entire forest, possibly even in the entire world.

The English Civil War had many a skirmish and battle around these areas as Gloucester, off to the north of the Forest, played a pivotal part in the history of the War. If it was not for Colonel Massey holding out in the siege of Gloucester the history of Britain may have been vastly different. One of our haunted buildings is Littledean Hall, possibly the most haunted private house in Britain.

A contemporary report states:

"Lieutenant-Colonel Congrave, Governor of Newnham, and one Captain Wigmore, with a few private souldiers, were surrounded in some houses by the residue of our horse. These had accepted quarter, ready to render themselves, when one of their company from the house kils a trooper, which so enraged the rest, that they broke in upon them, and put them all to the sword..... Congrave died with these words, 'Lord receive my soule!' and Wigmore cryed nothing but 'Dam me more, dam me more!' desperately requiring the last stroke, as enraged at divine revenge."

We can then jump forward to the time of Nelson as there is a statement of Lord Nelson's relating to this Forest, written about the year 1802, in which he says:

"Nothing in it can grow self-sown, for the deer bark all the young trees. Vast droves of hogs are allowed to go into the woods in the autumn, and if any fortunate acorn escapes their search, and takes root, then flocks of sheep are allowed to go into the Forest, and they bite off the tender shoot."

The Forest was important militarily throughout its entire history, it being a source of wood to build ships, coal and iron. These mines have played a massive part in the shaping of the Forest as a community and the mining work even continues to this day with a few haunted mines that we will be visiting throughout this book.

So let us stop this history lesson and get on with the ghosts. I will endeavour to tell you a little of the history of each place that we visit, but only enough to put it all in context for you, as this is after all a ghost hunting book. So grab your torch, and let's look for spooks.

CHAPTER 1

ROYAL FOREST ROUTE —
PART ONE

The first section of this book is about a walk or drive around the Forest called the Royal Forest Route, maps of which can be downloaded; it features many tourist sites that are haunted, as well as haunted roads, so I will take you along a small part of the route in this first chapter, between St. Briavel's Castle and Coleford.

You may want to plan a day around these sites starting with dinner at the Georges Inn, followed by a walk around the Clearwell Caves and Puzzlewood, ending up in Coleford for the evening.

St. Briavel's Castle

I am going to mention very briefly at the start of this book my favourite haunted location of all time, which is St. Briavel's Castle. I am not going to tell you too much about this place just yet as I will go into great detail about an ongoing investigation that I have been part of since 2006.

The reason I am putting it at the start of the book however is that it is a youth hostel and is a very good way of staying in the forest very cheaply and experiencing all the haunted locations that I am going to tell you about.

So if you were to look up on the internet any ghost stories about this location, you will find three that occur again and again, so I shall briefly tell you of these but leave the rest for later as there is an entire chapter on the castle.

There is the ghost of a crying child in the King John's Lounge area of the castle. There is a White female figure that roams the first floor, and for those of you not going to stay at the castle for the night you may be lucky enough to see the ghost of a knight in shining armour that stands near a fireplace against the wall of the castle, and can be seen in the grounds. If you walk into the castle and turn left you will see a fireplace against the outer wall, which used to belong to part of the castle but has since fallen down. The ghost has been seen in the day, so feel free to wander into the grounds and see if you can see him. If you can't see him then head over to the fireplace and have your photo taken whilst placing your head into the replica stocks they have built there.

If you are staying at the castle you can eat there quite cheaply or you can head into the castle moat where you will find the George Inn.

COLEFORD

Puzzlewood

Perrygrove Railway

Sling

B4431

The Miners Arms

Clearwell Caves

Clearwell Castle

Brookhollands

B4231

BREAM

B4228

The George

St. Briavel's Castle

Don't worry if you can't follow my map; you can always download a copy of the Royal Forest Route for free.

St. Briavel's – The George Inn

I do know a few stories about the pub, and during one of the ghost nights at the castle that I help run we had a talk from a previous landlord about how he got so fed up with the ghost on the upper floors of the building, (as he could not sleep that night because of the noise) that he ended up confronting it and shouting at it to get lost and leave him alone.

It is a fantastic little pub, and a glorious piece of Forest history; well worth a visit even if you don't want to go ghost hunting as I have had many a delicious meal there before a night of spook watching.

I have spoken to landlords and staff within the building and they all seem to get on perfectly fine with the apparition now though, and have even named him (not too unsurprisingly), George. Apparently George has taken a shine to the new management, and all is well. He only seems to misbehave when there are people there that he does not like, and so far the new management does not seem to have upset him.

Dena Bryant-Duncan talks about the George in her little book about Forest haunting called *True Ghost Stories of the Forest of Dean*. Whilst having a meal at the pub she needed to venture to the 'ladies'. As she walked through the door of the toilets she felt as though there was something else there with her, and as she went up the stairs she felt as though something was going to push her in some way.

The entrance from the car park to the George.

An excellent place to refuel on your day of spook hunting.

The coffin lid set into the wall at The George Inn.

When she returned to the bar area one of the regulars in the pub asked her if she had seen anything up there? They then proceeded to tell her a tale about their mother who saw a Cavalier in full period costume. The landlord then laughed and told her the place was full of ghosts.

Apparently the building is built over an old footpath and the ghosts do not realise that it is not a footpath anymore and keep wandering through.

One rather amazing sight in the pub is a stone coffin lid, and it is well worth visiting the pub just to see this. If you walk in through the car park entrance of the pub you have the bar on your right; now go around the corner and look back at the bar and the full length of the wall where you will see a stone coffin lid with an old Celtic style cross on it. The very helpful lady behind the bar told me that it was found when doing building work under the pub. It is not the only thing under the pub as there are many tales of tunnels leading from the pub under the moat to the castle; we have yet to find them in the castle though.

The coffin lid was set into the wall of the bar, and the body was reburied under an orchard in the village. Perhaps it is the ghostly figure of this person who frequents the bar. He seems to have been a monk, and has appeared as a full apparition staring at people in the pub, moving things, and making noises particularly on the upper floors.

Brookhollands

There have been some rather strange and weird phenomena, within a small little hamlet between Lydney and Coleford, that has more than its fair share of spookiness, and paranormal attractions. There have been many witnesses to strange goings on, including a visitation from another world, not the spirit world but one of a more Stella variety, a visitation by aliens. In the year 2000 a local farmer claims to have witnessed a bright circle of lights surrounding his farm. Unfortunately, as with all fantastic events there was not a camera to hand, and the lights flew back into the stratosphere.

Perhaps the aliens had been scared off by one of the Forest's big cats, one of which seems to have a prowling area, around Brookhollands. I will talk more of the big cats later on in the book, and talk about my conversations with the big cat expert of the Forest, Mr Danny Nineham. The cat around here is supposedly a black panther, and may have been an escaped pet, or zoo animal, but locals think it may be responsible for killing domestic cats, and sheep.

The ghosts are no stranger to Brookhollands either as there is apparently the ghost of a burglar to be found. I guess it is bad enough having to get up and investigate bumps in the night in case they are burglars. When you find out that it actually is a burglar, that is rather terrifying, but when the burglar then disappears in front of your very eyes, it has to be worse. I am not sure if there would be a sense of relief or even more terror. He was apparently killed one evening whilst trying escape into the garden of number 14. There also seems to be the spirit of a murder victim, whose body was discovered in the Forest back in 1999.

A fishing farm also rose up from the spot where a World War two bomber attempted to kill off a few Foresters. A German bomber was flying over the Forest and had to dispose of its unused cargo of bombs, so decided to drop them on Brookhollands and the enterprising Foresters turned the crater into a fishing farm.

Paisley House – and The Mizen Family

Back in October 1969 the Mizen family moved into the area and they lived in the house know as Paisley house, one of two houses built by a local tradesman and builder way back in the late nineteenth century. The reason for the name was because of the large paisley pattern that the roadway was carved into, and he also built paisley villa before running out of money and scrapping the whole project. It is a shame that finance stands in the way of these great visionaries; we may have ended up with a whole paisley village if he was slightly richer.

Well Mr and Mrs Mizen spent many a sleepless evening as they were repeatedly woken up throughout the night, by the sound of something resembling muffled heartbeats. They walked through the entire house trying to source the strange noise and could hear it everywhere they went. Eventually they called in the environmental health officials and their equipment detected the sound, but the operators could not offer any explanation at all.

Sling – The Miners Arms

There is only one thing I like as much as a gothic spooky haunted castle, and that is a haunted pub, because if you can see a ghost it is a good excuse for a quick shot of whisky to settle the nerves. Well, this little pub in the village of Sling has more than one landlady, the current living one and a previous dead one. Formally known as Old Nell, the ghost was officially renamed Elizabeth after she was identified as a former landlady from the 1880s. She is referred to as a friendly ghost, and has a tendency to move items around the building.

I went along and checked with the staff at the pub to see if there had been any recent activity, and was told that ever since they had added an extension the activity had died down a great deal. This was quite an active spirit and would even be strong enough to move chairs around in the bar. This is also a prime example of how altering the building can alter the activity of the ghosts; sometimes it makes them more active, sometimes less so.

One of the best things about this pub's ghosts is that one of them can be identified and this is very rare. If you want to see what she looked like head into the bar and sit in the very comfortable area tucked away on one of the sofas, as there are several photos of her here. You could even sit in their restaurant, have a fantastic meal, and see if you get served by a previous landlady.

Clearwell Caves

There is a fantastic tourist attraction called Clearwell Caves which unsurprisingly is just before you hit the village of Clearwell.

Like all tourist sites in the Forest of Dean they can be seasonal so please make sure you check their website or call them for opening times. On their website it does give many reasons why you should visit, so I will tell you what they say.

- Nine impressive caverns open to the public
- Atmospheric caverns and passageways
- Lots of great things happening; see our events page
- Caving activities
- Blacksmith workshop
- Ochre workshop
- Educational and fun for the whole family
- Guided tours for pre-booked groups
- Gift Shop with excellent souvenirs, gifts, crystals and minerals to buy
- Spectacular Christmas Fantasy event in December
- Great cafe
- Surface walks
- Picnic areas
- Ample free car and coach parking

I could not disagree with a single item on here, it is a fantastic afternoon out, and if you really want to get involved then go on one of their deeper cave explorations. I would like to point out that I am not in any way receiving any sort of commission for singing the praises of the caves, it is just that I have had some great times there. I thoroughly recommend going at Christmas time as you may be lucky and get to see Santa as I know he likes going there as well.

It is clearly signposted, just follow the road around until you reach the car park. Walk down the steep small path until you get to the entrance and I would say head into the mines before you read the book, so that I can tell you the tales after you have seen them, if you experience anything for yourself.

If you are the kind of person that wants to know what is in there before you go in then please read on.

The history

As well as entering an extensive natural cave system and mining museum, when you walk around underground remember that in Clearwell Caves you are experiencing some of Britain's oldest underground mine workings, dating back thousands of years into the Stone Age. The Forest area is known for its iron ore, and has underground and open caste mines dotted around, particularly in the Clearwell vicinity. Where there is iron ore then ochre can be found as a by product, and many a forester has made his living mining for these. The ochre occurs in powder form; red, yellow, purple and brown ochre, which are highly valued as pigments and still mined at Clearwell Caves.

One enterprising miner went to America and saw that the local Native Americans painted their faces using ochre, and from his forest experience realised that where there is ochre there is iron ore and so set about mining there. Not only did he become a millionaire he also named the area, 'The Forest of Dean'.

Like some of the other mines in the Forest you can still meet the occasional free miner, men whose ancient birthright entitles them to dig for minerals within the 'Hundred of St. Briavels' and the Royal Forest of Dean. Basically, if you are born here you have the right to try and be a free miner. There are very few of them left in the Forest nowadays.

The main mine and museum entrance.

I do need to explain what free miners are at this point as we will meet them again in another haunted mine called Hopewell colliery. So I shall use someone else's words to help us understand.

> "All male persons born or hereafter to be born and abiding within the said Hundred of St Briavels, of the age of twenty one years and upwards, who shall have worked a year and a day in a coal or iron mine within the said Hundred of St Briavels, shall be deemed and taken to be Free Miners." *Extract from Dean Forest (Mines) Act 1838.*

The next question I hear you ask is, "what is or are The Hundred of St. Briavel's?"

Although its origins are not totally understood, a Hundred became a subdivision of a County, a division that had its own court. One theory is that it was an area where the medieval king could demand the services of a hundred fighting men, under a baronial system of government – The St. Briavels Hundred, would have demanded of it, the services of skilled miners. Today the Hundred of St. Briavels area consists of the statutory Forest of Dean and each parish touching the Forest boundary.

One of these free miners is called Jonathan Wright, and he now manages Clearwell Caves and says that he is the last Free Miner still mining iron ore and ochre. Jonathan's

The fake mine entrance near the café in Clearwell Caves.

On a sunny day a beautiful place, to sit and hopefully talk about the ghosts you have just seen in the mine.

family have mined within the Forest for many generations, with many of his family members being Free Miners as well, including his father, Ray Wright, who in 1964 formed the Royal Forest of Dean Caving club.

The Ghosts

So what spirits do we have lurking around waiting for the unwary visitor to the museum to find?

Well one of the old stories about the mine is that it is inhabited by at least one old miner who is still down there working away. In the 1970s, a television crew was making a documentary and filming in the caves, quite deep in the mine. Unfortunately they had to stop filming as someone walked across the set. This was rather infuriating and someone approached him to tell him to leave the set, yet he carried on regardless. This annoyed the crew so they decided to forcibly remove the intruder and the old miner turned and walked straight through the man from the film crew. This was unnerving enough but they also saw a bright light appear at the far end of a tunnel, so they all sat there and watched as the light got brighter and larger, and it headed towards them. The light then all of a sudden went out leaving them in the darkness of the caves illuminated by only their camera equipment.

I do not think it is any stretch of the imagination to think that these people may have been a little on the scared side, and as the story goes they left a lot of equipment down there in their hasty escape. One of the technicians even ended up with a badly injured hand as they ran out of the caves.

The reputation of the haunted caves soon spread, and a group from the Rank Xerox Company in Mitcheldean decided they would be brave and check out the stories. According to Sue Law's excellent little book on forest ghosts, they went down the mine at six o'clock armed with torches and a camera. To them it was just a fun night out, and I do not think that they were expecting anything to actually happen. They were a few hundred yards into the mine and down two or three levels of mine workings when it all happened.

They had decided to settle down in this area, as it seemed as good as any other part of the mine, when the man holding the camera shouted,

"It's true!"

Apparently he then backed away, falling over in the process and breaking the camera. They looked up and saw a yellowy orange glow heading towards them from the back of the cave; they claim that it looked like a figure carrying a candle. It passed across the rock face about twenty yards from where they were, and then they described the sound of a few 'chinks' on the rocks like someone hitting it with a pickaxe. The team left all sense of decorum and bravery down the cave and ran out as fast as they could.

This is not the only film crew that has had a ghostly encounter in here, for Doctor Who has visited a couple of times. A cave is not an easy place to film, as cables need to be laid and lights have to be set. The crew needed to run cables from one area of the mine to another, and they were trying to work out how best to do this, when a helpful miner pointed out that they could run a cable through a hole and it would lead to an area they needed to get to, cutting out a great deal of work in the process. They thanked him and later when talking to the people in the mines they asked who it was that told them to run the cables in that direction and no one knew who they were talking about. It's always nice when a ghost gets a good reputation for being helpful as there are far too many nasty ones spoiling it for the rest of them.

This ghost may be the one that helps tourists and children find their way out when they are lost in the caves, and has been reported often. I remember when I was a youngster and my parents used to take us out to interesting places in the Forest and the Cotswolds, a habit that parents of today do not seem to do, instead replacing a great walk through amazing places like puzzle wood with a trip to an out-of-town shopping centre instead. To these people I say life is short and this world is a glorious place so go out and enjoy it; a trip to Clearwell Caves, Puzzlewood, or Perry Grove Railway are a fraction of the price of designer clothing, and the memories will last forever, long after the colours of your clothes have faded.

Another ghost hunting group brought some night vision camera equipment into the caves and managed to film strange misty figures walking around, and strange Balls of Light floating through the caverns. We brought a large group of visitors into the caves with all their equipment and even though they saw interesting unexplained phenomena all fifty of them failed to get anything on camera, as per usual the cameras all point in the wrong direction at the wrong time. One thing you have to be aware of when using these night vision cameras is that they can pick up dust very easily, and appear as floating orbs in front of the lens, so obviously in a place that has ochre powders and dust in it, it is likely you will get strange orbs appearing. One group were down the mine and heard metallic tapping responding to them calling out to the ghosts; it is thought that it may have been a 'miners knocker' where miners would hit a metal bell or plate, to signal to workers in another area of the mine.

I was lucky enough to be able to speak to Jonathan and he told me of a story that had happened to him back when he was younger. He was using a large drill and hammering away at the rocks, when another miner tapped him on the shoulder and motioned for him to lift the drill up. Immediately Jonathan knew what the miner was indicating, as it meant that he had been drilling into the rock at an angle and curving the drill, which is a very costly mistake to make as the drill will become jammed in the rock. He dutifully lifted the drilling equipment back into a better angle and thought nothing of it. It was not until later when he was talking to the others at the mine that he asked who was the guy that came down earlier. None of the others knew what he was talking about; Jonathan thought they were winding him up. This man had been wearing proper mining attire, so he assumed he had been sent down to check on how things were going. To this day no one has owned up to being the helpful stranger.

It seems as though we are talking about a collection of ghosts in these caves; they may all be miners yet their descriptions vary in time and costume. Some of them are barely distinguishable from a miner that would be down there today. Others like the one that the group from Rank Xerox saw were carrying candles and pick axes as though miners from a time long gone. Whoever they are let's hope they stick around for a long time to come to delight and look after many more visitors to this fantastic tourist attraction.

Clearwell Castle

Unfortunately Clearwell Castle is not open to the public; well, not officially. Its main function now is as a wedding venue so I guess if you want to get into this place you need to persuade them that you want to get married there. They may become slightly suspicious when you ask to take photos in night vision, and pull out thermometers, EMF meters, and Thermal imaging hardware. Be warned though, the staff there do not like talk of ghosts, and have turned away many a group before. At one point in the history of the castle the owner rebuilt a staircase to stop one of the ghosts walking up and down it. There are also a set of doors that have been known to open and close of their own accord when no one is touching them.

It is a shame that you can't get into this building as it tells a great story. There is a figure in a red dress that haunts the castle, another figure that sits in a window seat clad in a beautiful silk dress, and one bathed in exquisite perfume, (this may actually be the same ghost), and hooded figures which walk the corridors of the castle. This figure may well have been seen by several rock legends. In the seventies the castle was used as a recording studio, and greats such as Freddie Mercury and Black Sabbath have stayed here. It is Black Sabbath that gives us this next tale.

The main Gateway into Clearwell Castle.

Way back in 1974, Black Sabbath were having a problem recording their new album so they decided to get into the mood by staying and recording at the castle. The eventual album that came out was Sabbath's fifth album, "Sabbath, Bloody Sabbath."

They had been struggling to write the album, and in the castle they recorded the title track and a great sense of relief came over the band thinking it was all going to be fine, now they had found such an inspirational setting for their work. Unfortunately the Sabbath did not feel as though they were alone in the castle.

They rehearsed in the dungeons there and one evening they had been setting up equipment when Tony Lommi and Ozzy Osbourne walked out into a corridor; there they saw a figure in a black cloak. They followed the figure back into the armoury and saw nothing, so whoever it was had disappeared into thin air. When they questioned the castle's then-owners they were very matter of fact about it, and said that it was the ghost and they had nothing to be worried about.

Apparently the rest of the sessions were ruined as they kept trying to scare each other by rigging up elaborate pranks, and they eventually scared themselves so much that they drove home every night instead of staying at the castle, which defeated the purpose of being there altogether.

The second entrance into the castle.

Puzzlewood

I have included Puzzlewood in this collection of stories, not because I have heard any amazing ghost stories about the place but because I thoroughly recommend that you go there if you want to get into the spooky vibe. I have heard tales about Roman ghosts being spotted in the area along with ghosts of miners, but nothing that I can pin down to a particular haunting. So, whilst there, keep your eyes open as I need more information on these elusive spirits.

What you will see when you are there is one of the most best kept secrets of the British countryside, a truly magical place that looks like it must have been built to film *The Lord of The Rings* in it. Indeed it is rumoured that J. R. R. Tolkein himself visited the woods. If you are near a computer, on the internet go onto the You Tube website and search for the place, and you will see videos that have been added that show some great pictures of this treasure.

The strange natural pathways and unusual features seem to stem from an underground cave system that through geological shifts was forced to the surface where the top layer of rock then became eroded leaving the chasms and causeways.

Fellow ghost hunter Dave from PARASOC investigating Puzzlewood on one of the coldest ghost hunts I have ever been on.

Puzzlewood is beautiful any time of the year but is particularly stunning, and slightly treacherous to walk through, in the snow and ice.

Head to Perrygrove at Hallowe'en for the Ghost Trains – Photo courtesy of Perrygrove Railway.

In 1848 when some workmen were in the woods and moved a block of stone, they found a small cavity in the rocks. Within this tiny cave, they found treasure in the shape of three earthenware jars and inside were over 3,000 Roman coins. So perhaps the rumoured figure of a Roman ghost is actually looking for his money after investing it all in Forest Rock, probably safer than Northern Rock I suppose.

Perrygrove Railway

I have also included a very brief section on Perrygrove Railway, as it is very close to Clearwell, and like Puzzlewood at Hallowe'en they run a kids attraction, The Hallowe'en Ghost Trains. Thoroughly enjoyable, and something you can do if you are ghost hunting with the whole family.

Coleford – Angel Hotel

The Angel Hotel in Coleford claims that it may be the most haunted pub in the whole of the Forest. A landlord of the establishment known as Ben Fullwood has reported many a strange occurrence. He claims that they have a poltergeist in the establishment, as he has witnessed glasses falling and smashing all of their own accord. He also reports of showers that turn themselves on without anyone touching them. The hotel guests are not the only guests that stay at the hotel as it seems that there may be ghostly visitors as well. One guest left in the middle of the night as they felt someone get into the bed with them; we are assured that there was not actually a real person getting into the bed, so it must have been one of the ghosts.

This is not the first time that the dead have visited the Hotel as in its history back in the 1600s one room was previously used as a mortuary, and the alcohol that was flowing through the building was actually in the embalming room.

Ben has reported that the incidents got so bad that he had to keep the lights on so that the cleaners did not get spooked in the mornings. During further research we even find out that the ghosts are not confined to inside the building. Cavaliers have been known to knock on the doors, so if you are in the area and you have a wicked sense of humour turn up wearing a cavalier outfit and see how many people you can terrify, unless you get scared off by the ghosts of the roundheads marching from Gloucester through the Forest.

Coleford – Police Station

Coleford police station may be an intimidating building, but Sue Law tells us in her book *Ghosts of the Forest of Dean*, now reprinted by the Forest book shop in Coleford, that the building should scare you. It was built in the grounds of an old house. Late at night the officers would complain of footsteps heard in the corridors, yet when examined and investigated there would be no one there. They had a ghost that did not like doors to be left open; if the interview room door was left ajar then it would close it before you returned. The most unpopular room seems to have been the interview room, and they all seem to think there is an unpleasant atmosphere in this area.

One theory is the 'stone tape theory' that a building can retain memories of events that have happened, and I am guessing that an interview room is not going to have seen many nice events in its past. The Forest has to put up with its fair share of vehicles ripping through it, and in the summer many a tourist on his motorbike will be zooming up and down the hills. Yet it seems a ghostly tourist may stop outside the station as the sound of a motorbike pulling up in front of the building is heard, even though there is nothing there.

A police station I assume is a building where you need order, and you do not want things happening that cannot be explained, yet there are countless stories of unexplained noises, footsteps, creaks, and even doors being slammed.

Coleford – The Coombs

The Coombs is an old Victorian house that was used as a residential home for the elderly. Back in the nineteenth century, Isaiah Trotter, who was the owner of Oakwood chemical works (and not a yellow three wheel reliant van with Trotter enterprises written on the side), lived there.

He was a landowner around this area back then owning large expanses of the Forest. He had a great sense of public duty and built alms houses and catered to the poor. A female member of his household actually killed herself as the story goes through shame. She fell in love with one of the stable boys, and after an affair she became pregnant, but because of his lowly status they were not allowed to marry, and the shame she brought on herself and her family drove her to hang herself in the stables.

The story jumps forward now to the 1970s, and our witness is the deputy matron who lived in the grounds of the old house. The events seemed to start from the moment they moved in, as they would hear odd noises throughout the house. The front door would rattle and yet when opened there would be no one on the other side. They would also hear someone walking into and through the house from the back door, and then through the kitchen. Voices and laughter were heard outside getting closer to the door until someone tried to open it, but when the person in the building opened to the door to let them in there was no one there.

The milkman was even a witness to the events at the house, as he rang the doorbell one day asking if they had a ghost, as apparently a white figure had rushed in front of him and disappeared. They seemed to think that this was the ghost of the Trotter girl (as in a female member of the Trotter family, and not a girl with pig's hooves just to clear up that image for you). They thought this as when they did some work in the garden they found the foundations of the stables, and it seems that their building was on top of the route she would have taken from the main house to the stable block to see her lover.

The ghost itself seems to take on many different attributes, as she has been known to scream, talk, laugh, and play jokes on people. She has also been known to push people when they are not looking, and when the staff are getting ready and washing she has been known to dunk their heads under the water into the sink.

My favourite story about the house comes from Sue Law's book of *Forest Ghosts* and tells how one visitor had a snowball thrown at them from out of thin air. The ghostly activity, we are told, died down a few years later when more building work was done. This is often the case, when buildings undergo alterations it seems to wake up the ghost, and when it is over their activities go down again.

For all we know perhaps they are interested and are coming along to see what is being done with their old place, or perhaps they are somehow recorded in the walls and the action of the builders is releasing their pent up energies. As investigators with the paranormal investigative group called PARASOC we are often called into a building just after it is renovated, and we actively seek out old buildings that we know are about to be rebuilt in some way. Partly this is done because it is the best time to see a ghost, but also it is sometimes the only way we can get to investigate old hotels as the guest get a bit scared when they bump into us in the corridors carrying cameras and ghost hunting equipment.

CHAPTER 2

ROYAL FOREST ROUTE —
PART TWO

Parkend – Fountain Inn

The Fountain Inn was an intriguing little nugget of ghosts that I found whilst researching on the internet, so my hopes were high when we headed into the Forest to visit. Like all Forest venues they are not necessarily easy to find, so it is always worthwhile looking at a map first. This one seemed to be on our Royal Forest Route, so it should be easy to find. Ben and I drove slowly through the village, annoying the locals behind us who assumed we must be tourists by the speed we were going at, and eventually we thought we must have gone past it. Unfortunately, we were two men in a car, so we did not want to ask for directions; Ben eventually gave way and demanded that I ask the two people stood next to the post office where we were supposed to be going.

He pulled the car alongside the road, and told me to ask for directions. I refused being the man that I am, but also because I could see the pub over the road. It is an attractive old building opposite the old railway line; things looked promising so we stood outside and took a few photos, before heading inside. We were in for a treat as this is a gorgeous little bar in the style that you want a country pub to be in, with stone walls, and various strange objects hanging from the ceiling. We closed the door behind us noting the particularly nice stained glass in the door, and headed for the bar. We had not planned to drink I must add, but instead we were going to ask about the possibility of Ghosts.

"Excuse me, I am researching for a book on haunting in the Forest of Dean, I was wondering if this pub had...." Now before I could finish the sentence the rather useful woman behind the bar butted in with, "Well you have come to the right place", and so we had; not only was this pub haunted, but they also had very usefully kept records of the haunting going back several years. This was the perfect publican's publication presented to persistent ghost hunters; everywhere we go we are told stories of vague recollections of something that happened to someone once, and then you ask someone else in the bar and they give you completely different 'facts'. So these people were our dream come true, stories that could be verified and checked.

I asked where in the building their ghost was, and the reply was perfect:

"Which one?"

Be on the look out for big cats, and don't forget to download your free Royal Forest Route map from the Forest Tourist Information websites.

It transpires that the pub is full of them, so let's start with the diary. The diary itself is thousands of words long, and I could fill the book just with excerpts from it, so I will stick to a few that illustrate the haunting. I asked if we could publish sections from her diary and she said yes so I will let the landlady explain in her own words.

'The Fountain Inn Ghost Diary'

There are many other things that happened before I started the diary, the things I remember are a lady in Room 1 saying she heard someone walking outside her room then tripping and falling heavily, on investigation, no one was out there, also footsteps reported outside Room 7 but again the corridor was empty and so were the other rooms in that wing.

I also saw a woman in the mirror of the disabled toilet stood behind me, I remember she had shortish dark hair.

At the time I was feeling unwell and was due to start my journey to visit family in London, I decided to have a sleep and see if I felt any better before I travelled and just as I was about to lie down I saw someone standing by my bedroom door, I put my

Note: that's my reflection in the mirror just in case you thought I was a ghost.

Sit in the window seat if you wish to get prodded by the ghosts.

head on the pillow and suddenly realised what I had seen, sat up again and the person was still there. As I laid back down I thought to myself someone is trying to tell me something, so I decided it would be better if I travelled the next day. I subsequently felt worse over the course of that day and realised that if I had taken the trip I would probably have been a danger on the road.

The next day I travelled safely to my family and my mother and sister returned with me to stay for a few days.

In the morning while we were stood in the kitchen making breakfast I suddenly turned and saw a figure stood watching us, it quickly disappeared.

It made me feel as if whoever it was, was saying, "See, if I hadn't stopped you travelling that day you wouldn't be standing here with your family now", Ever since this happened I have always felt protected by whoever is still here in the pub and this is why I decided to keep a diary of the unusual things that have happened over the years.

Saturday 17th January 2004
7.30am Kitchen
A large serving spoon hanging on a hook started to swing, it was surrounded by other spoons that did not move. The windows and doors were closed and no fans were running.
8.45am
A laminated A4 notice in the corner by the dishwasher flew horizontally off the wall landing in the middle of the kitchen floor, again, no doors or windows were open and no fans were running.

These are great examples of simple poltergeist activity. We asked the Landlady if she had a background in paranormal research, to which she replied that she had a passing interest, especially with all the activity in this building, but we ascertained that she was not an expert. So the fact that her story of the A4 notice travelling horizontally had more believability to it than expected. Most people who do not research paranormal beliefs would not know that poltergeists tend to throw things horizontally and not in an arc shape; you will see more about this when we visit St. Briavel's Castle.

This diary is also a great example of details. We are told that the other spoons were not moving, and that they were adjacent to the moving one. This would rule out draught, and vibrations, as it should in theory make all the other spoons move as well. Hopefully we will get in to investigate and that will be on my list of experiments to try out.

When we arrived, the woman behind the bar told us that she did not feel scared at all when she was in the cellar, so I would like to point out that not all haunting are scary. I have witnessed full bodied apparitions of figures in period dress, or even only half a figure stood in front of me, and I have not been scared. I have also been in a well lit room, and heard the slightest, tiniest noise and been petrified. The haunting itself denotes whether or not you should be scared, and not what it looks like. On that note I will show you another entry a bit later on from the diary.

Sunday 7th March 2004
2.25pm
A small boy in a royal blue top was seen passing the bottom of the cellar stairs

Are you sitting comfortably? Then we shall begin; ghost hunting that is. Welcome to one of the most haunted pubs in the whole of the country.

Now the great thing about this story is that it happened in the cellar, most pubs have cellars, and there is normally only one way in or out. Most importantly there is very little capability of getting into a pub cellar without someone knowing, so this sighting is unlikely to be of a real child that wandered down some stairs.

Monday 8th March 2004
10.00pm
Smell of extinguished candles behind the bar

Tuesday 9th March 2004
7.00pm
Smell of flowers behind the bar

Friday 26th March 2004
12.30pm
Smell of burnt toast outside Room 8

Wednesday 31st March 2004
7.00pm
Smell of pipe tobacco outside Room 8

I have included these four entries as a lot of paranormal activity is not visual; it is often reported as smells and sounds. Some people will read these stories, and say 'well, perhaps someone had burnt some toast, or someone had been smoking tobacco outside room 8.' We have to assume that the Landlady probably also had these thoughts and checked these ideas out as well. Too often, sceptics come up with a possible explanation for a haunting and say 'well that is what must have happened.' People who do this are just as guilty of self deception as the people who walk around believing in everything. To be a true paranormal researcher you have to have an open mind, but not too open that your brain falls out.

Wednesday 31st March 2004
11.50pm
Figure of a man seen walking in the bay window area, this was viewed from outside. The pub was locked up for the night and in semi darkness

We were told that the bay window area was somewhere where people often experienced paranormal activity. People sitting here have been nudged by unseen hands. This may be the same figure that was seen a few months later. So if you are planning on a pint or two, order from the bar and sit in the bay window, as it may be your best chance of a paranormal experience.

19th May 2004
Lunchtime
The bar maid and a customer saw a man stood by the front door but he disappeared in front of their eyes, later that afternoon another customer said he had seen the same thing, not knowing what had happened earlier

The interesting thing about this story is the collaboration of separate witnesses' stories. When we report on stories we only like to include tales that have more than one witness, and ideally witnesses that saw separate events that correlate in some way. Ghostly events tend to repeat or concentrate on certain areas and objects, and these next two entries are a perfect example.

7 July 2004
Evening
The kitchen was closed and staff had gone home. There was a clatter heard from the bar, when the bar maid went in to investigate the window hook was on the floor. The window was closed but the wind could not have blown it off as the wall fixing is a round hook. 5 Minutes later a mug 'fell over' no mugs were stacked on top of each other and they were stood in a flat tray. I told the ghost to stop messing me about because I was busy in the bar and no more was heard.

13th July 2004
Lunchtime
A mug inside the tray jumped out and smashed on the floor, no one was near it at the time.

We see here that the activity is centred around a certain part of the pub, both tales include mugs, and both happened within a relatively short time of each other. If there is some form of intelligent entity behind the haunting then I guess it is only natural for it to try and concentrate on a particular place or object hoping that it is easier to notice if something happens more than once. I am not saying that I believe in this theory, but if you believe in life after death and spirits trying to communicate with us then it makes sense to behave in this way.

Another example of repetitive behaviour happened again a few months later.

Thursday 28th October
Morning
During the morning shift a member of staff was in the dining room and saw someone in the bar walking towards the fireplace, upon investigation they found that nobody was there and the only other member of staff in was upstairs, this happened twice in one day.

There are many more entries telling more and more tales, often depicting apparitions that fade or disappear after a while. I have chosen this next one as a more interesting example.

Tuesday 11th December 2004
7.30pm
A customer was sat in the bay window when he saw the reflection of a woman in the window, she was in her 30s with short dark hair and wearing dark rimmed glasses. All the customers sat with him were male and he could account for their reflections, she stayed there for a few minute then vanished, the customer then disturbed by this got up and checked around the pub to see if anyone fitting her description was in the bar but to no avail.

The reason I liked this story was because of two aspects; one was the fact that the figure was a reflection, and the other was that the witness tried to explain the event through natural means. Ghosts are often described as a hallucination, sometimes a mass hallucination with several witnesses seeing the same thing at the same time.

There are sightings where four or five witnesses all agree that they saw a figure but their descriptions vary so wildly that it is hard to believe that they saw the same thing. One scientific explanation for this is that each witness is hallucinating, and that the haunting is not actually a physical thing stood in front of them, it is more that the brain is picking up on an idea of an image and then projects it into the witnesses' vision. This is one reason it is believed that it is so difficult to film a ghost as it may not exist anywhere other than in the minds of the witnesses. This is not to say that something paranormal is not happening, as many people will see something all in the same place at the same time, but it may be a personal interpretation of some form of idea that is recorded in the atmosphere, and so will therefore look different to everyone.

The fact that this image was a reflection may be interpreted in a way that suggests there was an actual physical representation of a spirit or entity with some form of light-reflecting substance. This witness was the perfect ghost hunter, as they tried to discount rational explanations before they jumped to a paranormal conclusion.

One aspect of writing down all these stories is that you can start to notice trends that would not be noticed if this was just an oral folk record of happenings. We have an ongoing investigation at St. Briavel's Castle that has been happening over the last four years and we can notice things that the casual guest may ignore. If every time someone stays in a particular room they hear a door open then it may be paranormal, but if someone stays in that room once they will probably ignore it. It is the regular occurrence of the same phenomena that really interests the paranormal investigator. These two examples, although months apart, may be related to the same haunting, and so it gives you the opportunity to look though your notes and see if there are any more correlations.

Saturday 9th October 2004
Evening
During the evening shift the door leading from the bar to the toilets opened and closed by itself, this was witness by 3 members of staff who were at the opposite end of the pub, while they were looking at it, the handle moved up and down as if someone was on the other side trying to open the door. One member of staff opened the door quickly and checked downstairs but there was no one there.

Friday 18th February 2005
5.50pm
Member of staff was opening up the pub when they saw someone walk through the toilet door by the fire place, then realised it was still locked shut.

Both of these stories relate to a toilet door. On planning an investigation with this information I would place a night vision camera facing this doorway all night hoping that we may replicate the haunting.

I include the next story as I hear this a lot about haunted places.

Friday 30 September 2005
1.30am
I was sat in the bay window in the dark as usual after locking up the pub when I felt someone's fingers drag across the top of my head.

One reason this may have happened is due to the fear response in humans, which dates back to when we were more ape-like. If we became scared then our hair follicles would react; this was done so that the hairs would stand on end and make us look bigger than we actually were, hopefully scaring off the attacker.

Whenever we get scared nowadays a similar thing happens, although we have evolved from the apes and so we are not covered in hair, but you can still see the goosebumps on your skin. This often feels like someone touching you on the top of your head, or can cause the skin to be itchy. I am not saying that this person did not experience anything paranormal, but the next step is to see if this happens on regular occasions in the same place, and if it only happens to one person then it may be that person is very sensitive to the prehistoric fear response.

I will not print the entire ghost diary here, but suffice it to say that this is something that happens again and again and may be some form of paranormal activity.

Friday 23rd June 2006
7.00ish
I was stood by the Pepsi dispenser pouring a customer a drink, when I heard someone coming up the stairs (the door was wedged open so I heard it very clearly) I moved to one side to let them pass me but when I looked up no one was there. My bar maid also heard the footsteps as did the customer who I was pouring the drink for.

I included this story because it illustrates that the pub has every form of activity; we started with poltergeist, smells, and apparitions, and finish with aural phenomena. Footsteps are a common form of haunting, and sceptics will often say that we are just hearing the sound of floorboards creaking as a building cools down, or warms up. For those of us who have heard these footsteps, let me tell you there is a definite difference. It is impossible to convince a true sceptic, but one sounds like a creaking floorboard and the other definitely sounds like someone walking on wooden floors.

The ghost diary continues with more and more items being added. We agreed not to print too much about what happened as we are planning on getting in there to investigate; the landlady says they often have people coming along to find the ghosts, so she would not want to give them any information before they get there. If you are a ghost hunter, I will tell you their ghosts have names which I will not yet divulge, and there are specific events that happened in certain rooms that may explain some of their hauntings.

The idea behind this book was to tell you about places that you could go to and hopefully experience a real life or real dead ghost. Well this is an excellent example with a cheap youth hostel style bunk house out the back of the property, and you can even stay in style in a four poster bed in a haunted room. If you do stay and experience any paranormal happenings make sure you tell the landlady and please make sure you contact me, so I can update the records as well.

In my next book on the Forest ghosts I hope to be able to include an update with our PARASOC groups, investigations and more entries from the ghost diary.

Parkend – The Woodman Inn

The Fountain Inn may be one of the most paranormally active pubs in the Forest, but do not forget there is another pub just down the road called 'The Woodman'. It does not boast as many ghosts to my knowledge, yet I have been given some excellent reports about some poltergeist activity seen here.

We are informed that one intrepid ghost hunter even saw milk bottles floating around. There are other reports of small objects moving, and in an empty room stones have been heard to land on the floor. A previous member of staff has said he does not like the 'function' room, and gets a particularly eerie feeling when he is in there, and strange banging noises have been heard emanating from this space. One previous member of staff even claims to have held a séance in this room, and that they heard quite a few strange noises. I personally have not managed to get time to investigate these claims myself, but hopefully will be heading that way very soon. (I do prefer these haunted pubs to anywhere else, particularly when they sell cider).

Speech House – The History

Many people wonder why this building is called The Speech House, which dates back to as early as 1338. The Verderer's court of attachment was usually held at Kensley House which stood in the centre of the Forest, and the court held there was held on 'Speeches Day'. This house was continually used for the court, and over time became known as the 'speeches court' right up to the early seventeenth century.

Now you are probably asking yourself the very same question that I did at this point.

"What is a Verderer?"

Whilst taking this photo the author nearly became a ghost when he realised it was a silly idea to stand in the middle of the road to get a close up, especially when he had a zoom lens.

I got excited thinking I had found a grave opposite the Speech House, but in reality it is more like a commemorative plaque.

The impressive statue above the entrance of The Speech House.

Well, they are very important people by all accounts, as they were originally part of the judicial, and administrative organisations governing the vast areas of English forest, set aside by William the Conqueror for hunting. The name Verderer comes from the French word 'vert' which all us GCSE French language students know means green. Apart from the word for 'Hello' and 'My Name Is' I think that is the sum of my vast extent of French language skills. There was a Chief Justice who dealt with the major offences, and Verderers who dealt with investigation, recording minor offences, as well as day to day forest administration.

In 1676 this site was where Speech house was erected, and what we see now is the result of that build. It was decided back in 1669 that a house was needed to cope with *'the keeping and holding of forest courts for the preservation of vert and venison, in accordance with the laws of the Forest in pursuance of the Act of 1668.'*

So with an old building like this we can be sure of a good haunting or two.

The Ghost

One ghost investigation group reported when they were in there that they were trying to get some responses from whatever ghost was wandering around in there. Whilst they were trying to get some form of response a few of them were sat around a small table and the table started moving of its own accord. They thought it may be something to do with the fact that they were touching the table and moved their hands from the table top and it still kept on rocking backwards and forwards.

Other groups have reported moving glasses sat on tables, when no one appears to be touching them at all. For the avid experienced ghost hunter then there are also reports of orbs being seen on night vision cameras when this activity happens and near the objects that are moving. When you look at the history of this building it would be more unusual for it not to be haunted.

Some ghost hunters have contacted the building before and been told that it is not haunted, as is often the case some managers of hotels do not like their hotels getting a reputation as a haunted venue, as they think it may affect business, so you always have to look a little deeper. When a hotel can boast that a certain King Charles the Second has stayed there I guess it likes to keep its upmarket reputation regardless of how long ago that was.

Beechenhurst Trust, The Nagshead RSPB Centre, and Alien Big Cats

Some people reading this will think, why did I include a section on big cats, or alien big cats as they should be referred to as? The 'Alien' aspect being that they should not be roaming around this country and not the fact that they come from Mars.

There is a reason I have sent you to the Beechenhurst Lodge to tell you about big cats as it was not far from here that I saw one. This is as good a place as any to see one, partly because if you do not see a panther stalking you, you can at least go on the forest sculpture walk which is always fascinating, and a truly uplifting, marvelous experience. Should you not wish to visit here, you can visit the 'Nagshead' which is a nature reserve run by the RSPB; you can look for birds in the picnic area and hope to catch sight of a big cat as they have been reported by the bird watchers there.

One night Paul Tudor from the Cheltenham based PARASOC ghost hunting group and I were returning to Cheltenham from an eventful night of ghost hunting at St. Briavel's Castle. As we drove home through the dark, what can only be described as a black panther ran in front of the car and through the trees on the other side of the road. We both remained silent for about ten seconds, and then both of us said, "Did you see what I just saw?" We both replied in the affirmative and explained that we had both seen a panther. Bruce was driving the car and claimed he did not see anything as he was looking in the rear view mirror at something else at the time. We were rather scared as we were not sure what would get us first: the large black cats roaming the forest looking for food, or Bruce's dangerous driving.

I decided a few days later to try and work out what this creature was. I had heard tales of escaped zoo animals or private owners who released their pets into the wild but I could not be sure so I called someone who seemed to know more about the subject than I did. His name was Danny Nineham. For those of you who do not know Danny, he is the self-professed expert on the subject of alien big cats; you may think he is a little mad and that he is chasing shadows, as I get this about ghost hunting as well. Yet when you listen to him talk he is a man that knows his subject very well. I asked him, if there are so many of these creatures wandering around out there, then how come no

The Climbing Tower, a rather weird looking structure at Beechenhurst.

A close up of the notice board showing species and creatures spotted at the nature reserve, I hope this is a panther and not just a little black cat wandering around.

Ben getting excited looking for Big Cats at the NagsHead nature reserve, either that or just looking strange. I'm not sure which would be the most scared to see the other, Ben or the Panther.

one has taken a credible photograph of them? Danny at this point produced a rather large collection of A4 laminated photographs of panthers, cougars, mountain lions and various species of feline that I have no idea how to pronounce or type.

"You mean pictures like these?" I nodded as I had seen one that looked exactly like the cat that Paul and I had both seen.

"I have given up showing them to the press as all they do is want to sensationalise it or ridicule me." This is very reminiscent of every ghost hunter's experiences with the press; we cannot blame them as they are they want to sensationalise things to sell copies of newspapers, but they often do more harm than good. He gave me a sheet that he hands to policemen and school children about how to recognise different paw prints, and what to do if you spot a cat. He has even advised the government and the army on these matters. He told us a story about how quite recently he had been called into a school as a big cat had been seen staring at the playground watching the children playing. He seemed to think that the cat was staring at the children like it would stare at a heard of antelope or zebra, working out which one was the weakest to pick off for dinner.

I asked him what had got him started on his quest for big cats, and it turned out that he was also interested in ghost hunting and had dabbled quite a bit in the subject himself, yet he said that when he came across so many reports of big cats then this was something that was provable as opposed to hauntings. I have often said that even though I believe in ghosts I think most are explainable as physical things, and problems with how we perceive the world. Yet a big black panther walking around in your garden is something that is definitely provable and has a decent believable explanation to it,

Speaking of walking around in your back garden, a friend and ghost hunting colleague of mine used to live not far from here, and she once spent a rather enjoyable half an hour watching a rather relaxed mother panther and a collection of baby panthers frolicking around in her back garden. As per usual with all sightings of any credibility the camera was not to hand. I always say that no one has ever been harmed by anything paranormal, yet in the case of these out of the ordinary sightings I offer a word of warning: steer clear of the cats. If you are in your car or a safe place then quietly observe them but just because these cats are in this country do not think they are tame. A few years ago all the sheep in the Forest disappeared due to foot and mouth culling, so these cats had to get over their natural shyness and head into towns and search through bins for food. This lead to the breakdown of their fear of humans, so they are less scared of you than they used to be.

In our quite small collection of ghost hunters, myself, Paul, and Emma have seen these cats. We were talking about them at St. Briavel's Castle one day and a guest expressed his disbelief at them; another of our colleagues, called Sarah, arrived and walked through the gates and we turned to her and said, isn't it true about the cats in the forest? She replied that she had seen one on her way home from the castle at four in the morning as she drove past Hopewell Colliery.

A mining wheel in the car park and not all that is left of a stolen Giants Bike.

Make sure you visit Hopewell on a dry day – it can get damp in that mine.

Hopewell Colliery

We have had a few investigations into this fantastic little working mine museum. Hopewell Colliery is open to the general public in the spring and summer months; unfortunately the mines flood in the winter and it can be very damp down in the lowest parts. Paul and I ventured down into the mine and had a fascinating tour given to just the pair of us as we looked around to see if it was worthy of an investigation. We went down there just before spring so a few parts had running water going through the mine, but nothing that made it impossible to walk about. Well, nothing that made it impossible for me to walk around; Paul on the other hand is rather tall, and did hit his head a few times, but thankfully they supplied us with hard hats before we went down there.

Our helpful guide told us a few tales of ghosts, and that his favourite was when he was in the mine with a colleague and they heard another miner heading towards them, along a straight part of the mine that came in from one of the entrances. They thought it would be funny to hide around a corner and wait for him to walk past and jump out on him; the footsteps carried on getting louder towards them, and then when only a few feet around the corner they stopped. The pair of miners were trying not to laugh

The forest looking desolate and scary during one of the coldest winters we have ever had. Ghost hunting this year was a rather chilly occupation.

or make any noise, waiting for him to make those last few steps around the corner, and nothing happened. After a while they thought it was strange so decided to take a look, and nobody was there. These were both seasoned miners and knew what underground noises to expect, and in their minds they both knew that someone or something had walked down that corridor.

CHAPTER 3

LITTLEDEAN

Littledean Hall

Unfortunately one of Britain's most haunted houses is no longer open to the public. It used to be and when it was a fair few ghost hunters got a chance to find out what was happening in there. I will not dwell on these stories too much as it is immensely frustrating to know of a great ghost story and not be able to examine it firsthand. There have been people on this site for thousands of years, as recorded history tells us it dates back to a Roman religious site, having been a shrine before it was a house. Now the Romans, like the Christians, came along and instead of destroying religions that went before them they incorporated them into their own religions and we are told that the site was originally a Celtic shrine to the river goddess Sabrina.

Certain sections of the house even date back to Saxon times in the fifth century, and the Guinness book of records has declared that it is the oldest continuously occupied house in England; perhaps we should add another world record – that of the most haunted house in England as well.

There are many different forms of haunting in this great building including screams, clashing swords, pistol shots, rappings, and slamming doors. Do not forget that ghosts can also take on the form of smell and here we have 'olfactory phenomena' such as odours of decaying flesh, burning toast, and roses.

It seems that the most active ghost is involved in a plot to rival any Eastenders episode. Charles Pyrke lived in the Hall, as the Pyrke family resided in the hall for over 200 years, possibly longer if the reports of haunting are anything to go by. Charles Pyrke was murdered in 1744 by a young servant after having discovered that he was the father to the servant's sister's illegitimate child. The ghost of the servant has been seen on many an occasion since, outside his bedroom as well as in the drawing room.

Another ghost seems to frequent the dining room, as a Monk is said to walk from there to the library. The reason it is assumed he makes this journey is that there is a priest hole which led to a tunnel from the cellar to the grange of Flaxley Abbey. This allowed the monk to visit secretly to give Holy Communion. We have investigated many a house that has a secret priest hole, and it makes the point that religious extremism is not far from the history of most countries. Many a church or religious centre houses more than ghost, many of whom were put to death for their beliefs.

There are many stories of ghostly miners throughout the forest, perhaps some of our ghostly friends now walk this way to glimpse at the monument to them.

We may be a much more relaxed country now, but you may not get much sleep if you are staying in the Blue Bedroom. Previous occupants have said that the room had an oppressive atmosphere, and they would hear what sounded like a swordfight. If this is correct it would connect very easily with a sword fight that happened between two brothers, who killed each other in a fight over a young lady. There is a dark stain on the floorboards that could not be removed, it is said this is where the blood stained the floor. The floorboards were evenly sanded down, and still the blood stain returned; eventually these floorboards were replaced and the blood stain managed to return once more.

It seems the previous occupants of this house do not like to leave, as one of them, Richard Brayne, who lived here in the sixteenth century, has decided to stick around and do a spot of gardening. Richard appears as a gardener on the drive way. I wonder if they have to pay him; I am sure that working after death constitutes as overtime.

Some ghosts are not necessarily attributable to any particular person, and there have been, over the years, many reports of strange poltergeist type of activity. There have been various chairs, tables, and wall hangings that have been mysteriously rearranged and overturned. There may be a gardening ghost, but indoors there seems to be a ghost that may suffer from hay fever as flowers in vases have been found shredded and tossed about. The ghosts may also have a physical presence and not the type that can just drift through a wall as many doors open and close on their own initiative. What often happens with regular poltergeist activity is that you will have moving objects that get hidden and only return a few days later in a different place, and to my delight this building is no exception to the rule.

There seems to be a physical interaction between the ghosts and people as well. One of the residents of the house tells of an incident where he was awakened one night by the noise of his dog barking ferociously. He got up fearing that there was a burglar but immediately he was shoved by an unknown hand sharply in the back. Now as an investigator it is possible to jump to the conclusion that in his haste to sit up he pulled a muscle or two in his back giving the impression that he was shoved, but this is cancelled out by the fact that he goes on to tell us that he was then forcibly shoved across the bed. Before anyone asks, of course there was no one in the room at the time. He is not the only person to be affected in this physical way, people have reported dizziness, nausea, and strange sensations in the house but one of my favourite tales is from Avril Sumners who worked at the house.

Back in 1993, Avril was in the tea room, (part of the old stable block) when a strange black mist, that appeared to be sparkling in some way, came through a crack in the wall in the corner of the room. She claims it looked at first like a chiffon scarf, and then it formed into a large cloudlike mass and engulfed her. Terrifying as this sounds you would assume that she ran screaming from the building, but no, she just stood there, and we would like to applaud her bravery. We would do if it was not for the fact that the reason she stood there was because she could not move, she tried to but was paralysed; she cannot recall how long this lasted but did remember being pushed out of it, as if pushed by a person. Unsurprisingly this is the one experience that she claims is the worst one at the house.

The Bridge

Let me tell you a tale of a little field, down by the little bridge, in the little village of Littledean. No, it is not the opening of some strange children's story from Cbeebies, this is a ghost story instead. There is not just one ghost here but two, as two ghostly women are seen walking together on the field. Two bodies were eventually discovered by workmen who were working on the road, and the sightings have died down a little since.

Littledean House Hotel

In my mission to show you haunted places to stay and investigate we came across a perfect little hideaway, that being the Littledean House Hotel. It has its own stories of haunting and has had investigations from several paranormal science groups. More importantly is the fact that you can stay here and within walking distance are several great haunting places. You are only a ten or fifteen minute walk from the excellent Littledean Jail, so if you did not get to see everything one day you can visit the next as there is bound to be something you missed.

Littledean House Hotel.

If you are staying then watch out for Fred the ghost who haunts the landings on the upper floors. I asked the owners of the hotel if they had experienced anything recently, and they said they personally have not, but they have had reports from people staying there. There have also been paranormal groups in to investigate and found various phenomena such as moving lights and unaccountable noises.

Littledean Jail – Crime Through Time Museum

The history

The Crime Through Time Museum is situated in the Littledean Jail building, and is actually inside the cells and courtroom. It was designed and built by the revolutionary pioneer of prison reform, Sir George Onesiphorous Paul, which has to be one of the greatest middle names of all time, and leading Prison architect William Blackburn. It was completed in 1791.

This building was so good in its time it was later seen as the Government's model for Pentonville prison in London, and then later was the design used for Cherry Hill penitentiary system in Philadelphia. It cost a small amount by today's prison standard coming in at a mere £1,650. This budget was not necessarily a good idea as building work was started in 1788 by Gabriel Rogers, who went bankrupt not being able to complete the work at such low costs. Another builder, J. Fentiman, was brought in to finish the job within budget.

The Crime Through time Museum has to be one of the most fascinating buildings I have ever been in. My PARASOC investigation group were going to do an evening of ghost hunting here, so I decided to go along and see what the place was like. It is amazing, it is full, and I mean full to bursting point, with amazing objects all in some way linked to crime, the macabre, and bizarre world we live in. It includes some scary looking goblets made from human skulls. Andy, the owner of the jail, says that he only wants authentic objects in his museum. He claims that when he went along to a witch's coven meeting just outside Bream and saw blood being drunk from these skull cups, he decided there and then that he had to have them.

You could write an entire book just on the objects found in this museum, from the thousands of signed photos of celebrities that have been involved in some way with crime, to electric chairs and used hangman's ropes. The rooms dedicated to the Prisoner of War camps in Germany are a truly harrowing experience, and one that I think all of us should at some point be made to contemplate. 'Man's Inhumanities to Man' are shown repeatedly throughout the museum, where various torture implements hang from the walls, through to full sized gibbets dangling from the ceiling.

Printed on one of the doors is a small sign that states:

"IS THERE ANYBODY THERE? IT HAS BEEN CLAIMED BY MANY PERSONS AND PSYCHICS (THROUGHOUT THE YEARS) I HASTEN TO ADD NOT BY ME! THAT LITTLEDEAN JAIL BUILT IN THE YEAR 1791 IS ONE OF THE COUNTRY'S MOST HAUNTED HISTORIC PROPERTIES. APPARENTLY THE GHOST OF A YOUNG CHILD STILL WANDERS AROUND THIS CELLBLOCK AREA – DAY AND NIGHT. SPOOKY!!!"

It is this reason that the owners became interested in paranormal groups investigating, as Andy (the present jailor) and his wife had heard children running up and down the corridor on the first floor. They do have children and live above the jail, but knew that they were all accounted for. Other groups have gone up the stairs to the night cells and heard the same noises. When we investigated, it was this floor that seemed to hold the most in the way of strange feelings and sensations.

Unfortunately when we investigated we did not come up with much in the way of evidence of haunting. This is not because the building is not haunted, but more because we spent most of the night looking at the exhibits. We do an experiment called sensory mapping where everyone involved in the investigation would walk around and say out loud, (but not within earshot of anyone else) any strange feelings or sensations that you get whilst walking through a building. This is done by everyone and later on comparisons are made. When I went to look through all the footage of these sensory mapping experiments, all I saw was footage of ghost hunters all being fascinated by what they were reading, and looking at.

I challenge anyone to go to that museum and do a serious investigation because the place makes it so difficult, it is TOO INTERESTING! People have reported seeing children in the building, and in its history children have died here, at least two babies died in the cells. So if you do see a child make sure that there is not a school party in before you start screaming at it.

Let me leave you with a few words from the Crime Through Time's website:

"On one occasion the experience became so intense that one paranormal investigation climaxed with a fear of unusual and incomprehensible events; from museum exhibits shaking, lights flickering, and ending with complete loss of power! The group were last seen heading towards Cinderford screaming their already decapitated heads off!!!"

CHAPTER 4

OTHER FOREST VENUES

If you are staying for some time ghost hunting in the forest here a few venues that are just a short car ride away from our central royal forest route that can be visited.

Goodrich Castle

I do love castles and the forest is full of them. Thankfully I do not think there is a castle in Great Britain that does not have a ghost story attached to it; I think it must be a prerequisite for being called a castle.

The area of the Forest is full of stories about the Civil War, partly because Gloucester played such an historic part, as without the famous siege of Gloucester failing the history of this country could have so easily been very different.

The Civil War affected the country in many different ways and Goodrich did not escape. The war split the country, the towns and cities and even families taking up arms against each other. Two young lovers from opposing sides of the war tried to escape the whole affair so that they could be together.

On the royalist side there was a young Cavalier known as Charles Clifford who was based inside Goodrich Castle, and on the parliamentarian's side was Alice Birch. Alice was the daughter of Colonel Birch who happened to be leading the Parliamentary forces besieging the castle.

Through sheer will and determination Alice managed to infiltrate the castle to join her lover; let's face it, even in war women are better than men. The forces of the army besieging a castle and she manages to walk in. When the castle was eventually surrendered to the parliamentarians, the two of them fled on horseback through the Roundhead lines to the Wye.

Unfortunately the storm that had been so helpful in aiding their flight also made their escape very dangerous. The storm had swelled the river that they needed to cross, and as they ventured across they drowned in their desperate bid for freedom.

It is said that on stormy nights their cries can still be heard over the rushing river.

Tintern Abbey

Tintern Abbey can be found to the west of the Forest, and I would venture there on a nice hot day as it is a ruined abbey, so there is no roof I am afraid. Little remains of this once fantastic Cistercian Abbey founded in 1131. In the thirteenth century the building was massively developed, enlarging the building, which was completed by the end of the fourteenth century.

Even though Tintern is in a state of ruin it has been called the finest relic of Britain's monastic period. Surprisingly there are few stories around the ghost sites on the internet, and few paranormal investigators decide to head to Tintern. It is however a rather haunted site, for large numbers of visitors have seen the ghost.

Perhaps, as so often happens, they assume that the ghostly figure of a monk is actually of flesh and blood. So many ghosts may go undetected because people do not realise they are ghosts, particularly the noisy ones. If you are at home watching TV and your kids are running around making lots of noise, you may have the ghost of a tap dancing headless lion in your kitchen but you are not going to hear it over the noise of an *Eastenders* wedding, or an argument over who gets to play on the Nintendo Wii.

Mr. and Mrs. Cartwright of Sutton are two such witnesses; they saw the monk who was on his knees near one of the arches on the west side. They thought he was actually a monk and a devoted worshipper, but just as they were about to pass him, he vanished.

Raglan Castle

One of the last castles to be built in Wales is Raglan Castle. It was built between the years 1435 and 1525, on the previous site of a Norman Motte castle. It was built by Sir William Thomas, known as the blue knight, and by that I assume it does not refer to his love of racy rude jokes. The castle is a ruin, but a reasonably well preserved one, so well worth exploring, but beware – you may not be the only visitors on that day.

The castle plays home to a ghost from the Civil War period. Visitors have described what they call a 'Bardic' figure; he seems to beckon you to follow him to the area of where the castle's library was situated. It is due to this that he is thought to be the castle's librarian. He supposedly hid the castles valuable books and manuscripts in a tunnel under the castle when the Civil War headed their way. This was a well founded fear, for one of the first things that happened as the castle was raided was the destruction of Raglan's magnificent library. Knowledge, it seems, is always hated by those that wage war. The fate of this careful librarian is unknown, but he is still seen to this day, and schoolchildren on field trips have reported him; perhaps they were making too much noise in his library.

Even if you do not happen to see the librarian the whole castle seems to have an eerie air about it, and it is well worth an afternoon's visit.

CHAPTER 5

ST. BRIAVEL'S CASTLE

The History

I thought I would give you a very brief history of the castle so you can see how much history is packed into this glorious building, The castle is not in fantastic condition and has had several sections rebuilt; however it is not a ruin, unlike most castles in this country, as there is a great deal of remaining walls and building, but only a few fragments of rock from the castle keep, which collapsed in 1752.

It was mostly used as a replacement for 'Old Castle of Dene' (*vetus castellum de Dena*) which got a mention in a charter of Henry II to Flaxley Abbey. The history of the castle is sometimes somewhat obscure, and there are a few blanks that need to be filled in, but in its early years it fell, just like the Forest of Dean did, during the reign of Stephen, into the hands of The Earls of Hereford. It was not restored to the Crown until after the accession of Henry II.

It was most definitely owned by the king in the 1160s, but yet again we hit a dark patch as there were no accounts by the custodians of the castle and forest between 1164 and 1195. The story picks up however in 1197-8, when the constable claimed a massive sum of £5 that was spent on the castle and yet another similar sum was spent 1202-3 authorised by Geoffrey Fitz Peter.

King John was a visitor to the castle, and we know of at least eleven days that were spent here by the King. It seemed to serve him as a hunting lodge, and in 1209-11 a truly massive amount was spent: £291 12s. 3d.

The castle was not just a hunting lodge but also of huge importance militarily. It was the centre for manufacture and distribution of crossbow bolts; these were made around the castle throughout the forest, in the forges. This industry meant that the castle was looked after and kept in decent repair all the way through Henry the Third's reign.

Unfortunately the keep collapsed in 1752, and only a few fragments of it remain; you can see them in the grounds as just a couple of lonely rocks. The gatehouse, however, is still mostly remaining although many times rebuilt. It has a long passage flanked by half-round towers sitting on top of spurred bases, is characteristic of Edwardian military architecture, and has to be the castle's main strength. It was designed to be attacked from all sides even from within the castle walls.

From 1327 to 1331 the castle was owned by Queen Isabella, hence one of the rooms being named after her.

Ghost hunters walking in and out of the castle oblivious to all of the horrors that lie in wait for them.

Enter at your own risk, or stay at the Youth Hostel because it is a particularly great place to be.

The castle was owned at one point by Milo Fitz Walter. He had a particularly cruel son by the name Mahel, and at one point the castle had a disaster in the shape of a small fire which brought down a stone on Mahel's head and killed him.

During the Middle Ages, the Forest of Dean was divided for administrative purposes into bailiwicks and there were courts held at St. Briavel's Castle. Parts of the castle became at one point a debtor's prison, of which the 1832 Commissioners of Inquiry reported: "There is only one window, which is one foot wide ... and does not open."

There are also tales of how they executed people in the castle by hanging them off the front of the castle, sometimes there were many bodies dangling away as you walked into the building underneath them. It must have been a terrifying sight; if you ever came to the castle as a prisoner, you may have thought you may be next.

Throughout its history it has been used as a school, a munitions factory, a private house, a prison, and now it is a youth hostel. Below you will see a brief outline of it historical uses.

1100-1160 – Fort to guard Welsh Border
1160-1210 – Forest Head Quarters & Court
1210-1300 – Arms Factory

1300 –1485- Symbol of Royal Power
1485-1850 – Lawcourt and Prison
1850-1910 – School
1910-1945 – Private House
1945-Present – Youth Hostels Association
Royal Visits to St. Briavel's Castle

Henry II (1154-1189) visited in 1158, 1164 & 1179
John (1198-1216) visited in 1200, 1207, 1209, 1212 & 1213
Henry III (1216-1272) 1226, 1229, 1232 & 1256

Phantomfest

Now it is impossible to talk about St. Briavel's ghosts and ghost hunting without mentioning a small group I help run, called Phantomfest. They are a nonprofit making ghost hunting group, and unlike the other group I help run called PARASOC, this group has been set up specifically to run nights at the castle. Since 2006 this group has been

The original Phantomfest team Ross, Bruce, Paul, Emma, and Jenny.

running about ten nights a year of ghost hunting at the castle, and most of the stories you are going to read from here onwards have happened since then.

One important thing to remember about Phantomfest is that it is a nonprofit making organisation, and every penny paid to it goes straight to the castle or to the running of the event itself. This group started out of a need for cheap ghost hunting nights, as there are several groups out there who charge a lot of money, and we do not believe that a ghost hunting night should cost you any more than it would do if it was not a ghost hunting night. We have been called in to investigate many hauntings, and sometimes we have gone on commercial ghost hunts lead by other groups.

One rule to remember is that if, for example, a museum is haunted and it costs ten pounds to get in there in the daytime, then you should not pay more than about ten pounds to go on a ghost hunt there. The building is probably going to use very little in the way of things like electricity, as the lights will be off, so there is no extra cost there; also they do not need a large amount of staff, maybe only one to lock up or open the place, so they have no costs there. We have heard stories of places charging up to ten times the amount it normally costs just to be able to look for ghosts.

The average price for a ghost night at the castle is about thirty five pounds, which gives you not only a ghost hunt, but a bed for the night in a haunted bedroom, and also breakfast the next day. So as you can see bed and breakfast in a haunted castle for thirty five pounds is not exactly breaking the bank, yet there have been ghost hunters who have ended up paying over seventy five pounds each for the privilege of being there from eight at night until four in the morning, without a bed or food. Now when large sums of money like this are involved I cannot help but think that people feel they should see a ghost for that money, and that is when things like fraud may arise. I am not saying that particular group were fraudulent, but I was there helping out, and took the three organisers around the castle and told them where everything was. One of the people I was showing around was their medium for the evening, and I pointed out that not all the ghosts were indoors, as there used to be a castle keep which fell down about three or four hundred years ago, and that the fireplace on one of the walls was all that remained of the courthouse.

An hour later when all the guests had arrived I walked around with them as they told everyone all the ghost stories, and allowed the medium to do her magic. As we approached the fireplace she started to sense something, and amazingly she said she felt as though she was stood in a courtroom. These amazingly accurate revelations that she was sensing all seemed to coincide with the information that I had given them the hour previously, and also with the few stories that are available on the internet. I am not saying they were fraudulent; it was all just an amazing coincidence. So if you are going ghost hunting choose your investigative group wisely, and always try to go for a nonprofit making organisation.

Another thing to note is that you should always go into an investigation 'blind'. That is to say that you want to be uncontaminated of any information about the haunting. This group went round at the start of the night and primed their guests by telling them every story associated with the castle they could find. I also might add that the stories they had were very old, and had not been experienced for about fifty years or so. So obviously if you are reading this book I am about to give away all the stories. It may be a good idea if you are staying at the castle to stop reading now, spend the night here and then in the morning after you have hopefully experienced a rather restless, frightful, and sleepless night, then and only then read the book.

So if you are still reading I guess it must be the morning then, so may I take this opportunity to say good morning, and tell you that the castle often does an excellent breakfast. From here on in the story gets slightly scarier as I tell you about the years of investigations that Phantomfest have done at the castle. One major thing to note here is that we only write down stories that have happened on more than one occasion, or were so interesting that I had to write them down for you. There are hundreds of other reports that we have recorded but we tend to ignore them until they happen a second time to someone who could not have heard about the first incident, that way we know it is more likely to be a ghost and not an overactive imagination.

DO NOT FORGET that these stories occur regularly; these are not just one off events.

The Main Castle – Lower Floors

The Castle's Dog

If you are really lucky you may get to see the phantom dog that roams around the castle, he tends to be seen on the lower floors but also is seen many times around the castle and grounds. For some reason he tends to avoid the East Tower as he has never been spotted there.

One of our ghost hunters, Bruce, came to the castle for the first time and spotted the phantom hound yet never told anyone, as he thought that it was a real dog. It was later when another one of our ghost hunting pack looked rather scared and started talking about a dog, that Bruce realised it was not actually a real dog that he had seen. Other guests have also seen the dog and not said anything, thinking that it was real. Bruce and the other ghost hunter did not discuss what the dog looked like. Instead when they went home they found photographs on the internet of dogs that looked similar to what they saw. They then sent the photographs to one of the other ghost hunters so that it was independent, and neither could lie. They both picked the same breed of dog, which looked like a large Irish wolfhound style hunting dog.

The animal is often seen on the ground floor, near the area from the office to the refectory, walking along past the gents' loos, which I guess is useful if you get really scared then I suppose the gents' loos is a good place to be.

The Peeping Ghost

Two of our intrepid ghost hunters from PARASOC were the first to see this ghost. One night, at a ghost hunting Phantomfest evening at the castle, it was early in the morning and Jen and Emma were sat in the refectory. Footsteps were then heard coming down the stairs and along the corridor; they both looked up and saw a figure peer around the corner and look into the refectory, when the figure then retreated back behind the wall.

For some reason this struck them as rather odd, and so a silence fell between them, which meant they then realised that there were no longer any footstep noises. So, as the figure must still be there, they thought they would find out who it was. When they

GROUND FLOOR

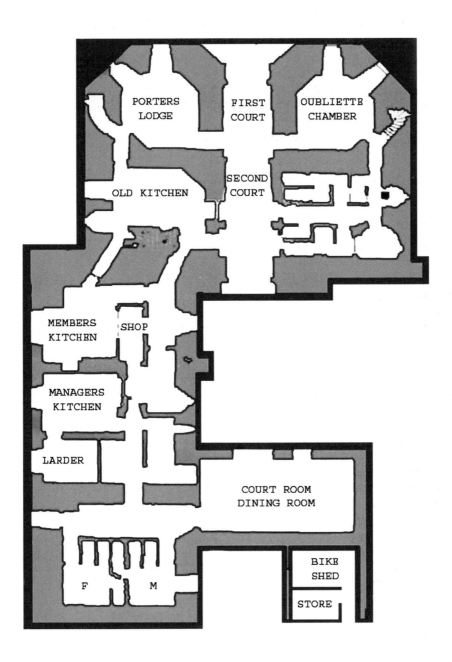

PORTERS LODGE

FIRST COURT

OUBLIETTE CHAMBER

OLD KITCHEN

SECOND COURT

MEMBERS KITCHEN

SHOP

MANAGERS KITCHEN

LARDER

COURT ROOM
DINING ROOM

F   M

BIKE SHED

STORE

Map of the Ground Floor of the Castle.

The face appears around the corner, but this door has also been known to open itself, and the ladies' toilets are just to the left of this door, also known to open by itself.

turned the corner fully expecting to see someone there was no one there. It had only been about ten seconds at the most between seeing the figure, and it not being there. If the person had walked off they would have heard footsteps, and doors opening and closing, if there had actually been a real person there.

A couple of months later I was sat in the refectory, and the group I was with had not been told about this figure. I looked at two of the guys who were sat chatting to me and they both were staring out of the refectory and along the corridor, just where Jen and Emma had seen the figure. I asked them what they were staring at, and they said a person had just looked round the corner at them and then retreated back behind the corner. They thought that for some reason he seemed a little odd, so we got up to check who it was, and when we looked no one was there.

This time they went up the stairs and I went the only other direction along the corridor, and through a door. I asked the group whom I encountered if anyone had just come through the door, and if anyone had been down the corridor. They replied that they had been sat there for thirty minutes and I was the first person to open the door in that time. When the other group returned from up the stairs they had similar stories to tell, this figure had seemingly disappeared into thin air yet again.

About five minutes later exactly the same thing happened again, this time I heard the figure as well; we heard some footsteps and then the other guys were in a position to see something. This time I expelled more energy than I have ever done before as I leapt over the table; I must have been standing where the figure had been seen within one or two seconds. Now even if the figure had ran up the stairs or down the corridor I would have seen him, yet there was no one there again.

This figure has appeared a few times since, and the footsteps are often heard going up and down the stairs.

The Footsteps on the Stairs

One such incident was during a Phantomfest ghost hunting night. A lady who had an injured leg (so was walking around with the aid of a stick) was sat on the bottom two steps of this staircase. She and her friend were casually chatting when they both heard the sound of someone coming down the stairs; it is not a wide staircase, so as this person got to the bottom of the staircase, her friend got up and she moved to the side to let whoever it was pass.

The sound of the footsteps carried on walking past them, yet that is all that was there, no actual person just the sound of footsteps, which possibly stopped exactly where the peeping figure is seen. I say possibly, because these two ladies did not stick around long enough to hear. It was an almost miracle cure as our injured friend seemed to be able to run again, both of them high tailing it out of the corridor.

These footsteps are also heard walking along the corridor. Occasionally, they walk from the old kitchen, past the office and towards the staircase; staff have occasionally reported seeing something out of the corner of their eye as they are working in the office, turning round to serve someone when they have heard the footsteps, and no one is there.

The Ladies' Loos

One of the more helpful ghosts is the one that inhabits the ladies' toilets. We went to the castle with a very inquisitive eight year old who thought that anyone who came there to look for ghosts and got scared was stupid. Fair enough, each to their own opinion I suppose. I was not going to tell her that I often get scared at the castle. She seemed absolutely fine walking around all the places, like the prison and oubliette, and not getting scared at all. It was not until she went to the toilet that she felt slightly unnerved. When she came back she said that she had trouble with the door. I assumed it was the metal bar that pulls the door closed, and it had not been oiled for a while making the door stiff. She then told me it was the opposite, as when she went to the door something helped her open it, to let her in. This has been reported very often, and the door will open of its own accord when there are people in there.

The Horses

Many a guest has been sat in the refectory, and the sound and smell of horses has appeared in the courtyard. You can hear the sound of the hooves on the cobbled stone;

The castle showing on the far left is the chapel window, underneath this room is the refectory. The other side of the small door is where the dog has been seen most often.

you can even hear people making noises as they lead the horses out. Suffice it to say there is never a horse in sight.

The Banging Noises

We always make sure that none of our guests are told the ghost stories until they have been there a good few hours and had a chance to experience everything for themselves; then we get everyone in the castle to group together in the refectory. Whilst we are sat down I talk about each room, and ask the guests if they have experienced anything in these rooms before I tell them what haunts it.

The groups then go through all the interesting things that have or have not happened to them. Every time we have been to the castle something has happened that defies explanation, be it apparitions, noises, lights, or poltergeist activity. Once they have given us their experiences we tell them the tales associated with that room, and nine times out of ten these match.

Up until now we have told people not to spread the stories around, and keep it to themselves, and we have successfully kept most stories off the internet, but it has now become a very popular site for ghost hunters and more and more stories are creeping out. This is the reason I am writing this definitive guide to the ghosts of St. Braivel's.

When we do this round up of tales, we are very aware of the fact that there is nobody anywhere else in the castle; we also have video cameras all over the castle to prove that we are the only people there, and that we are all sat down in the refectory. The last four or five times we have done our round up, we have been sat in the refectory listening to something move and bang around upstairs in the chapel. Each time the noises happen one of us runs upstairs to prove there is nothing up there, no windows open, nothing falling over etc, and each time there is nothing there. We have had video cameras in the room relaying a live picture, and we can hear things banging on the floor and see on the screen that there is no one there.

So, if you are now sat having your breakfast in the refectory, listen out and see if you can hear our friendly noisy ghosts above your head.

Slamming Doors

As is often the case when we do a night of ghost hunting with the general public invited along, we stay at the castle the night before to get base readings and investigations done before anyone gets there. Quite a few of the guests have realised this and tend to book in and come and join us for a more informal investigation.

The small ground level door leads to where we were stood watching the refectory doors moving and the latches opening.

One night we had the doors to the refectory closed and myself and Paul were in the old kitchen, and a few guest upstairs in the prison. We also had two other guests near the refectory and the closed latched doors. We heard a great deal of excitement coming from these guests and we all went to see what was going on. When we got there they told us the doors were unlatching themselves and opening. We continued to experiment with this and a few of us went into the refectory and a few outside in the corridor we then closed the doors, and watched them being rattled and latches moving. We knew full well it was not any of us or anyone else in the castle as we were either side of the doors. We even walked around trying to find draughts and gusts of wind that might cause it but to no avail. This continued for about five or ten minutes, died down and then stopped.

The Main Castle – Upper Floors

The Crying Baby

One of the most regular haunting stories you will hear about the castle is the crying baby. The internet is rife with ghostly tales of the Forest of Dean, yet when you actually start doing some research you realise that all these websites give you the same tales over and over again. Now the internet tells three stories about St. Briavel's: a knight in shining armour, a lady in white (both of which I shall come to later), and a crying baby.

The place that you are supposed to experience the crying baby is in the King John's Lounge. In all my time here I have not actually heard this spirit, or know of anyone else who has, but it has been heard in a few of the other rooms. Because the story of the baby is associated with this room however I will tell you about it as we go through the upper floors of the castle. The King John's lounge is so-called as he apparently had it built and slept in it. It is also called the solar room, as it had windows on every side, allowing you to have sunlight all day long.

Now an old tale states that late at night a baby would be heard crying in this room. One interesting twist to this tale is that when the castle was being refurbished years ago, the body of a baby wrapped up in blankets was found above the fireplace; since that grisly discovery the crying has died down.

Another problem with crying baby ghosts is that when you get town and city dwellers coming to places like the castle they are not used to the sounds of the countryside, and many a forest policeman will tell you they have been called out because someone heard a baby crying in the woods. Ninety nine percent of the time this is a fox; they can sound remarkably similar. The first time I heard it I was absolutely sure I could hear a child in a hedge in a school field in Cheltenham; thankfully I had a friend with me who lived on the edge of town and he explained it to me. Apparently police helicopters are often called out for this reason, and unfortunately every time they are called they have to check it out just in case it happens to be that one percent time when it could be real.

The Floating Lights

One familiar area of paranormal activity throughout the castle is the floating lights. When I say floating lights I do not mean there are chandeliers floating as if pushed by

FIRST FLOOR

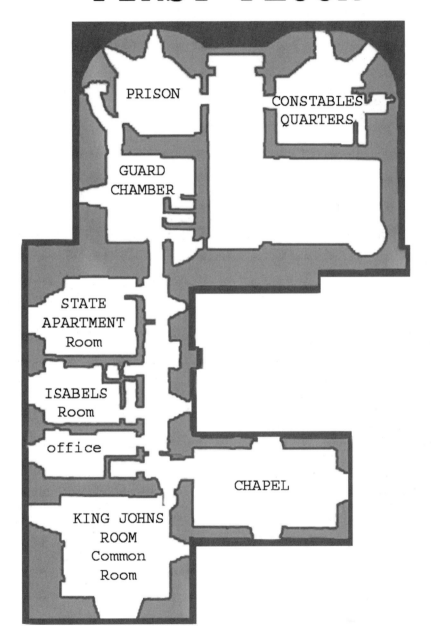

Map of the first floor of the castle.

Notches on the fireplace are supposed to indicate how many people were executed by one of the judges who used this room as a court room.

some unearthly hand, nor do I mean a one hundred watt light bulb floating around a room; no, these are strange floating light emanating balls of light, or BOLS as they are known in the ghost hunting world.

You may have heard of Orbs, or you may have watched *Most Haunted* and other such paranormal programs that will tell you the strange white orbs you capture on your digital camera and night vision cameras are the first manifestations of a spirit. However, pretty much all of the time these Orbs are dust, insets, or other floating detritus in the air, and can be recreated quite successfully in any dusty room. Now, do not get me wrong, some Orbs are fantastic, and we have filmed some that glow, fly around at incredible speeds and angles and seem to defy all laws of physics, but the majority are just dust.

Now BOLS on the other are much more interesting, because these balls of lights can be seen by the naked eye. You do not need sophisticated thermal imaging or night vision cameras for these, and we have amazing footage of these floating lights with people pointing to them proving that what they could see was actually there in the room with them, and not an after effect shown only on the camera screen.

BOLS can be any colour, but what is interesting is that in one of the rooms they are one specific colour, in another room they are another colour, and in this room they tend to be of an orange nature. The most regular place for them to be seen is near the glass cases with the maps in them on the wall; immediately on the right as you walk into the room. They seem harmless as they appear to float around for a short time and then just vanish or fade out.

Sometimes these appearances are very fleeting, and you have to remember that your eyes do play tricks on you. A split second glimmer of light may well just be the rods and cones in your eyes misfiring and playing tricks on you, but when these things float around for a few seconds they become much more fascinating. I wish they appeared more often, as the amount of people that forget to bring torches with them is remarkable, so it would be useful if the ghosts could supply BOLS to everyone as they walk in.

Smoke, Lights, and Ink

'It's all done with smoke and mirrors,' Agatha Christie would say and yes it is when it comes to magic. I often give talks in the King John's Lounge about fraudulent mediums and con artists, and the magic tricks they use to try and con you into giving them lots of money.

In all our years at the castle I am not the only person to give talks in this room. Paul and Bruce from PARASOC give an amazing talk on 'The Beginners Guide To Ghostbusting' which is invaluable for our guests who have never done anything like this before. We have also had Danny Nineham, the big cat expert, in the Forest, who spends all his time looking for the panthers and mountain lions that live in the Forest. People say there is no evidence for these creatures, yet the photos we have seen that he has taken are amazing. Stephen, the psychic artist, has come along a few times to the castle and given demonstrations of what he has done; we have other groups come along and give talks on their findings and research, and we often have CJ, a paranormal researcher, who has worked in TV, radio, and paranormal science all his life, and yes, that does include an occasional stint with the Living TV show *Most Haunted*.

CJ was giving a talk one day in the lounge, and several of the guests later reported that they could see what looked like smoke and lights from behind where he was stood, in the fireplace area. This has since been repeated on several occasions. Quite often as was the case in this instance the people witnessing the event are too scared of ridicule to say anything and it is not until later when one person has the courage to say something that all of the guests then claim to have seen the same phenomena but were too embarrassed to say at the time.

So, if you are on a Phantomfest night, never be afraid to say anything; you may think it sounds weird, but believe me we have heard a lot stranger than you could ever imagine. I often think that the stories we get to hear about are just the tip of the iceberg, and in reality lots of people keep all the best stuff to themselves.

There is another interesting visual phenomenon that happens in this room that has ended up being called the ink effect. It has been captured on camera a few times, and seen by a great number of people. Whilst sat in the room certain areas appear to get darker; no shape is attached to the effect but when you are sat with the lights out there is still light coming in from street lights, moon light, torches etc, yet the room will suddenly become blacker and sometimes this can spread to obscure your vision almost completely. We have seen many a photo taken during the night and day, where you can see this darkness spread, as if someone has spilt ink on a photo and it is spreading out across the image.

This strange effect has also been seen in the Prison room. Let us not rush there yet, as we have so many more stories to tell about this area of the castle.

Footsteps

We have already mentioned the sound of footsteps heard on the lower floors of the castle, including the story of people moving out of their way. At the top of this staircase are the chapel, and King John's Lounge. When guests have been in these rooms they have heard someone walk up the stairs, and then nothing. For those of you who do not know the design of the castle, once at the top of the stairs, you have to open a large fire door, and then immediately you have to open one of three doors in front of you either to the chapel, King John's Lounge, or into what was the Great Hall.

These footsteps arrive at the top of the stairs and then there is nothing else; no sound of doors, no sound of talking, no sound of the person going back down the stairs again, and when you open the fire door expecting someone to be there, there is no one.

There are more footsteps to be heard in the Great Hall. This part of the building is now split into several rooms, with the State apartments, Isobell's room, a long corridor, and a small staff room that is used when staff members have to sleep over. This is one of the oldest parts of the castle, and has a couple of stories attached to it. One of the more unbelievable stories is that a mistress of King John's was pacing across the battlements above this room and fell to her death; the rumours were that she was pregnant and that a figure had been seen pushing her from the battlements, and it is her that haunts this area. The story is highly unlikely and has probably grown up through myth and legend over time.

Let's face facts: it is not as if they had paternity tests back then, so if a King did get someone pregnant, as I am sure they often did, then he probably would not care less about the poor girl. More importantly the area where this incident supposedly happened quite probably did not have any battlements. So if our poor young pregnant lady was above the state apartments then we have to ask the question: what was this mad pregnant lady doing on the roof of a very tall building in her condition?

After saying all that it is true that this area has a female ghost, which I shall talk about shortly. A strange thudding nose like someone falling is often heard in the state apartments. In this area, footsteps are often heard, as they tend to walk along the corridor, but also in the state apartments. Isobell's room very rarely has any reports of paranormal activity; the only you hear of are noises that happen outside the room. So if you are looking for a decent night's sleep, this is one of the rooms you should ask for.

When staying in the state apartments it is not unusual to hear footsteps walk into the room, across the floor and head towards the curtains; if you are really lucky, you will get to hear the curtains being pulled back, even if they are already opened or not moving at all.

The worst bed, or best if you want to see a ghost, is the one directly on your left as you walk into the room; many people have slept there and heard the footsteps around the bed. I have heard of one person being woken up four or five times in one night by the sound of someone walking around the bed. A friend of mine stayed the night in this

What some say is King John's Throne – in reality it is likely to be a window facing out to the original exterior wall of the great Hall before the Gate House was added.

room; there were ten of them in total sleeping there, and when the others woke up they turned and saw him looking very pale, and asked if he was alright.

"I am never staying here ever again," was his reply and true to his word he has not. I asked him what had happened, and he said he had not slept as the footsteps kept him awake all night, as if something was pacing up and down around the bed.

In the State apartments the noise of footsteps, tapping, and shuffling around is more likely to happen outside in the corridor than inside the room. The problem with these ghosts is that quite often people will think it is actually someone outside, just another guest wandering around late at night. It is only when there are a few people in the castle, and you hear the footsteps knowing that you are all sat down in the room together, and no one else is there, that you realise it is another unearthly visitor.

Red Roger

I include this ghost as I was on another group's ghost hunting night and they told me of this well known ghost that has been experienced in the King John's Lounge, called Red Roger, so-called because of his head of copious red hair. They then went on to tell everyone about this figure and the way he makes himself known, which is to appear as a dark shadow or lights. At this point I was impressed, as we do have orange lights that float around in here; not only that but we also have a dark figure that has been seen near the fire exit. I thought these people are good; they do actually know what they are talking about.

It was at this point one of the more sceptical guests with this group piped up, and asked the question that if he appears as lights or a dark figure, how do they know he has red hair? The guide then said that their mediums had said he has red hair and that his name is Roger. I have a very big problem with information gleaned from mediums; if it is information that cannot be checked or confirmed in any way, especially as I have mentioned that this particular medium had already claimed information that I had given her was from another ethereal plane of existence. Unless I am a ghost and don't realise it.

No other group that has investigated here has ever reported a red headed figure, and neither have the staff. Yet, they have reported the floating lights and the dark figure near the fire exit.

Moving Chairs

There is an experiment called table tipping which Phantomfest do in the chapel. I hasten to add this group has a belief system that is completely neutral, they are neither believers nor non-believers. Therefore, they show people all sorts of psychic experiments and allow people to make up their own minds as to whether they believe in them or not.

One such experiment is the table tipping experiment, where people place their hands onto a table and it starts to move. The way the group do this is actually by using stools, not tables, which is done for practicality reasons more than anything else. You place the stool on top of a table and ask whatever is in the room to move the stool that you are all touching; it is a bit like using a stool instead of a glass in a Ouija board. Don't panic; we will come on to Ouija boards later.

I'm telling you about these experiments partly so you can try them for yourselves, but also so you do not become confused with stool tipping and this next story.

In the chapel and the King John's Lounge chairs have been known to move of their own accord. One group even witnessed a chair moving to correspond with questions, and moved on request. As with all amazing phenomena the group doing this did not have a video camera with them, and were so engrossed with what was going on that not one of them thought about coming to get a camera from us, in case they missed the action whilst they were away.

This story does tie in with the noises of moving furniture and banging that are heard downstairs in the refectory though.

Ouija Boards

As promised I am now on to the subject of Ouija boards. I have previously talked about them in my last book. *Paranormal Cheltenham* has a section at the back of the book about how to be a ghost buster and talks about all the myths about Ouija boards. I advise against using them not only because of any paranormal threat, but because I have only ever seen them work once in all my years of ghost hunting and paranormal research. I have seen many a person get far too worked up about them and get obsessed. I think the main threat from them is not paranormal, but mental. If you are the kind of person that has an addictive personality, avoid these things as they can become like a drug and you will become obsessed not possessed.

www.Phantomfest.co.uk

A B C D E F G H I J K L M N

Yes   No

O P Q R S T U V W X Y Z

1 2 3 4 5 6 7 8 9 0

An example of a typical Ouija board – to be used with caution.

With all that said when Phantomfest show people what Ouija boards are we make sure that nobody does these things in the bedrooms, because some people can become very scared and upset about the board. So this means that lots of groups do them in the Old Kitchen, the Chapel, King John's Lounge, and the Refectory. During one session the glass lifted off the table of its own accord in the chapel, and this was repeated about two months later in the King John's Lounge. It only lifted a centimetre or two, but there was no one touching it at the time. So, if you are going to take a drink into these rooms, keep a tight hold on it just in case it lifts up and flies off.

The Woman In White

I have mentioned in previous publications about a thing called stone tape theory, where a ghost is recorded in the walls of a building and, like a video recorder, someone comes along and 'presses play' and replays the images of the ghost. A lot of researchers believe in this theory as it negates any need to believe in a survival of death and an afterlife. One piece of evidence that may back this up is a fading ghost.

The windows on the first floor from left to right as we look at them. The tiny window one the left is the Guard room, then the State Apartments, Isobel's Room, and a small staff room, the final window belonging to The King John's Lounge.

There was a ghost in Hampton Court of a woman who had her tongue ripped out before she was killed and ran across the grounds bleeding profusely from the mouth screaming as she tried to escape. This figure was seen every night for weeks afterwards; the bright red dress she was wearing became a pink dress, and then a grey dress as the colour faded, and eventually a white dress, until the figure disappeared altogether, leaving just the sound of her screams, and footsteps.

This would seem to suggest that like a video recording that gets played over and over again, the image deteriorates. This may explain why we have a lot of footsteps in the castle and not as many sightings. One figure that has been seen is the woman in white, or a misty female form, that is seen and heard mostly in the Great Hall, and more specifically, along the corridor outside the state apartments.

She is thought to be the source of the footsteps that are heard; she taps on doors and walls, as well as shuffling along the corridors. She is more often heard and seen at the chapel end of the corridor and she has been heard to sigh when stood at that end. This may also be the figure that is seen walking from the door area of the state apartments across to the window, although this figure tends to be a lot darker, and more often than not is more like a three- dimensional shadow stalking across the room.

We also have reports of floating lights and the stereotypical BOLS; this time they are generally of a white colour, and tend to group near the chapel end of the corridor.

The Violins

A cleaner that used to work here had a wealth of information about ghost stories over the years. She told us that often she would go into the state apartments to clean, and as she got there she would hear the sound of violin music playing. At the time it did not seem too strange as there was a string quartet that used to come along and rehearse in the castle.

She would open the door fully expecting to see the quartet playing their favourite Mozart piece and instead found nothing; there was no one there. This is one of the rarer ghosts but I would love to experience this one for myself some day.

The Young Girl

Not only do we have a ghostly woman walking the corridors of the castle but we also have a young girl seen in the same area. One theory for this is why would a ghost be the age it was when it died? If you believe in an afterlife and that ghosts are spirits of people coming back after they have shuffled off this mortal coil, then I guess the spirit is ageless. Now, if a spirit is ageless, why would it not come back as any age? If I died and decided I was going to haunt somewhere, I think I would choose to look like I did when I was in my twenties; at least my ghost would have a much thinner waistline, and come to think of it, a lower hairline.

We can verify that there were no children in the castle when the ghost of the young girl has been spotted, as it was during the ghost hunting nights, and for obvious reasons we do not have under eighteen year olds in the castle when there are ghost hunting vigils going on. We get people asking if their kids can come along all the time; I wonder what parenting skills these folks have who think a child will be able to sleep after seeing a phantom hunting dog walking around, or watching poltergeists throw things around all night.

We have occasionally had under eighteens come along on ghost hunting nights but they were specifically designed for kids to enjoy, and it was not until the kids went to bed that all the really spooky stuff was talked about, and the Ouija boards appeared.

The Arguments and Fights

When I talk about arguments and fights, I do not mean that the paranormal science world is such a heated and opinionated one that we argue and fight all the time (but yes we do). What I mean about this haunting is that just inside the chapel end of the Great Hall on several occasions we have heard, and some people have recorded, the sound of an argument. You hear it when you are in the rooms off the corridor, or even on the other side of the door before you walk into the Great Hall, but as soon as you are in the corridor it stops.

I also need to tell you of another argument that happens downstairs, outside the toilets, near the refectory. I left it until now as it may have some relevance to the argument upstairs as well. Two previous members of staff were in the Male and Female toilets, cleaning. One of them was in the Mens' and one was in the Ladies', when both of them heard an argument or fight breaking out, just outside of the doors in the corridor. So, both came out, thinking the other person had got into a heated discussion with someone else who must have walked into the castle when it was supposed to be closed. They met outside the doors looking at each other confused and bewildered.

Lights in the State Apartment

We have heard tales of lights around the castle; thankfully, so that you can differentiate between the rooms, the lights change colour. In the Lounge we have orange, in the corridor we have white, and in the State Apartments we have a blue colour. The interesting thing about the BOLS in this room is that occasionally they also have a mist attached to them, and that they tend to float around a certain area.

So if you are sleeping on the bed closest to the door on the left hand side, as you walk in you might not need a torch; the helpful ghosts might illuminate the room for you to be able to read your latest installment of 'Harry Potter and the petrified Ghost Hunters'.

The Knocking

Paranormal activity, in my experience, is normally associated with strange sounds rather than seeing a full-bloodied apparition floating around and rattling its chains. One such sound is a knocking noise; in other hauntings that I have researched this tends to happen before a bout of poltergeist activity, and we have had our fair share of poltergeists within the castle.

For those of you who do not know what a poltergeist is, it comes from a German expression meaning noisy ghost. They tend to start off as noises and these get louder over weeks or days; this starts to manifest itself by throwing things around, and in extreme cases, levitating people.

Now we have never been lucky enough to witness fully levitating people but we have seen many things get thrown around seemingly empty rooms, and I have seen things like keys, stones and sweets materialise from thin air and land on the floor.

The knocking noises tend to be in the larger rooms, focusing more on the old kitchen and state apartments. We have spent many nights trying to replicate the strange phenomenon that occurs in the castle by banging things, opening and closing doors, walking along corridors, and moving furniture to see what noises it makes throughout the castle. Before you think you heard the tapping and knocking noises last night, bear in mind that the radiators do make knocking and tapping noises.

We have managed to rule out quite a few of these stories with this explanation, but if you are lucky enough to hear the knocking it sounds like someone hitting the wall with their knuckles, or the tapping can sound like someone outside the window knocking to get your attention.

The Phantom Pillow

This next story has happened only once, with a possible second similar incident, but it does tie in with poltergeist activity so I thought I should mention it to you.

During one of our ghost hunting nights, a group was in the state apartment's room 'calling out'. This is a term used to refer to the act of asking the ghosts to do something. Typically you will sit in a room asking questions such as, "If there is anyone or anything in this room, can you make your presence known to us, by appearing as some form of light, or noise". Other braver people ask questions such as: "Can you touch one of us, or throw things." Whenever I am in a group of the braver types who ask to be touched by ghosts you always hear one slightly scared voice from someone saying, "Anyone but me that is." It always amazes me how many people go ghost hunting yet don't actually want to see, touch, or hear a ghost at all.

There is one problem with calling out, as sometimes when you do get a response it can be very scary. One group felt as though something was there and it was 'freaking them out' so they decided to leave the room. They went into the corridor and closed the door behind them. They thought that they were being foolish and after all they were here to find ghosts so they decided to go back into the room. When they tried to open the door they couldn't; it was stuck, as though something was behind it. When they did eventually open the door, there was a reason it felt like something was behind it, and that is because there was. A pillow had somehow managed to come off of one of the beds and wedge itself under the door making it difficult to open.

Another instance of flying pillows happened when someone woke up because a pillow had landed on their bed; this was the bed next to the door into the room again. So, if you want a decent night's sleep, avoid this bed.

A similar flying pillow happened to a friend of mine when he slept in that bed, although this time it was because he was snoring too loudly and the friend of mine threw it at him.

Electrical Interference

Ghosts can often play havoc with electrics and wiring; the castle is notorious for electrical problems, but this may just be down to the fact that it is years old and some of the wiring is prehistoric.

That being said, we bring in lots of electrical equipment that sometimes seems to have a mind of its own. Very often, you will have people filming with cameras they know well, and have used often, yet the batteries will drain in a matter of minutes. This is normally just before some interesting anomaly happens. Torches can do the same, as brand new batteries in torches can drain in seconds and then we are thrown into complete darkness.

One piece of equipment that gets used often is an EMF meter which measures the amount of electro-magnetic frequency or field that there is in a room, and one such piece of kit used by a lot of ghost hunters is the K2 meter. This has an array of lights on it, so when it comes near a spike of electro- magnetic energy it flashes; the more lights, the stronger the electro-magnetic signal. It is also thought that ghosts can give off this field, and effect these meters; on several occasions K2 meters have been placed on the alcove in the wall in the state apartments and shown the very same phenomena.

The alcove in this room is actually a window and used to be on the outside wall of the building before the gate house was added. You can also see that the original floor

The beautiful castle looks inviting and friendly in the day – but by night it is a different story.

level would have been vastly different from what it is today, as the window's floor level is about four and a half foot taller than today.

When these meters were placed in the alcove the group 'called out' and the meter seemed to respond to their questions, flashing when asked to confirm if there was anyone there. The interesting thing about it being in that alcove is that there is a solid wall behind it made of stone, so no electrical interference could come through it, unlike a modern thin wall with wiring in it.

This experiment has been replicated throughout the castle, but it is in this room that the best results occur. Other rooms to try this out in, that give regular good results, are the oubliette room, although outside of this room is where the fuse boxes are for the East tower so beware of electric interference, and also the Hanging room. I will come on to these rooms very soon as they have some of the best and most regularly occurring ghosts.

The East Tower

At the front of the castle is the Gatehouse, added not too long after the stone buildings were put there. There have been fortifications for over a thousand years on this site, but the stone buildings date from around twelve hundred onwards.

A view of the imposing East Tower, the Chaplain's room is just out of shot at the top of this tower, on the first floor is the Constable's room, and on the Ground Floor is the very scary Oubliette room.

The East tower is accessible only through the one door at floor level; although the upper adjoining rooms have fallen down years ago, you can still see the places where the floors would have been, and where the portcullis would have slammed down trapping attackers in a killing zone within the gatehouse itself.

The Chaplain's Room

Footsteps

Yet again we get the sound of footsteps, heard so often throughout the castle. I was here for a recording for a radio podcast and had sat down in the Constable's room below this room, when I heard someone moving around upstairs. I commented that I could hear someone moving around upstairs but that we had another first time ghost hunter up there and it was probably her moving around.

Once we had finished our allotted vigil time in the rooms I went upstairs to see if this ghost hunter had seen anything; she had not actually seen anything, but had heard footsteps, from exactly the same place that I had heard them on the ceiling in the room below. I asked her if she had been moving around, to which she replied in the negative and said that she had been sat still and had filmed it all so could prove it was not her moving around.

People ask us if we do have footage of ghosts or paranormal happenings and the answer is yes we do; events like this are perfect examples but unfortunately completely useless as evidence, as any sceptic watching it will say we dubbed on the sound afterwards. To be truthful, the better the ghost footage the less people are going to believe it. If I had an excellent piece of film of a Cavalier tap dancing with the headless ghost of King Charles the First before disappearing then people would just say it is a fake, which has been done on Photoshop or video editing software. Suffice it to say that we collect the evidence for ourselves, and if people wish to believe it or not they can.

Another Dark Figure

I always treat reports of figures being spotted with some scepticism because it is the one thing we all want to see, so we are primed to see this even if it is not actually there. Our brains are very useful and also annoyingly inaccurate pieces of equipment; if the eye sees something it immediately tries to turn it into an image it understands, which is why we see faces in random patterns and shapes. The brain needs to be able to do this to protect us from predators, and allow us to recognise each other even in the dark.

So, when someone says they have seen a dark shadowy figure, then I do not question that they have seen a dark shadow, but the figure aspect of it can sometimes be very subjective. The best people to see ghosts in the castle are people who go here very often, such as us, or staff. It was the staff who told me of a dark figure that they have seen near the door. If you do see a ghost in a room, the one place you do not wish to see a ghost is stood in front of your only means of escape.

Children

I have told you of the sound of crying babies in the castle, but it is not a place just for upset children, it is also a place where children like to play. You have to remember that even though this castle was a prison and a place of execution, it was also a boarding school and a youth hostel, so a great deal of excited children have run around these corridors, and still do.

Teachers often end up going into the East tower to tell off their kids for running around and making noise, only to find that when they get there the children are all fast asleep and snoring heartily away. Certain school groups that come here only put kids in the towers and the teachers sleep on the other side of the castle.

It does not matter what room you sleep in; in this tower you may hear the children playing, in fact you do not even have to be in a room as they are heard running up and down the stairs as well.

Flashes of Light

I have told you of BOLS in the castle; there are also flashing lights, although we tend to not give these as much credence as they may just be optical effects where the eye adjusts to its very dark surroundings. Yet, when these lights are seen by many people at once, we know that it cannot be something to do with the dark, and instead is something that is actually in the room with you.

One night we had a group of eight or nine ghost hunters in this room. We have a rule that, if you are going to take a photograph with a camera that has a flash, you must say the word FLASH before you take the picture, to allow people to cover their eyes so that their night vision is not ruined.

Well, twice in this room a flash went off and nobody said the word, so someone in the group got up and turned the lights on to be able to tell off who was taking photos. It then transpired that no one in the room had a camera. Not only did this group see the bright flashes they also saw red BOLS flying around as well. It is nice to see that none of the BOLS are clashing with each other's colour schemes yet.

The Neck Toucher

The same group that experienced the flash and the red lights had someone in their group who later said that she felt as if something was touching or stroking her neck. This disturbed her slightly but she put it down to being scared. It was not until I showed her a copy of things that happen in that room, and showed her the copious amounts of recorded times that others had been grabbed or stroked on the neck, that she became upset.

Other people that have experienced this phenomena have also said that occasionally they have been grabbed, pushed, poked, and had their hair pulled.

The Rich Ghost

One of the ghosts here seems to have more money than sense. A group of ghost hunters were sat in this room, and were 'calling out' to the spirits to make themselves known. I do like it when this happens as I would love to see a group's reaction if a ghost suddenly appeared and said "hello, what is it you want?" I think the immediate reaction would be screaming and a need for new underwear, rather than any other response.

This one decided to roll a penny across the floor; we were obviously sceptical about this and thought that someone could have been playing a trick and rolled the penny to scare the rest of the group. All of the ghost hunters in that room, however, were adamant that not only had no one there done it, but that the coin came rolling from a part of the room where nobody was sat, so it could not have been any of them.

For those interested the date on the penny was 1891, and I have yet to find anything significant in the history of the castle for that year. For all we know the ghost was making subtle clues as to who he is, but if it's capable of rolling a coin, then surely it can pick up a pen and just write us a note.

The Bedhopping Ghost

The castle has many bedrooms and they are all dorms, with a minimum of four beds in Isobell's room to a maximum of twelve in the chaplain's room. In theory, we can sleep twelve people in this room, yet it seems sometimes there is more than one in a bed.

We have had many reports of people lying or sitting in bed and they feel as though someone is sat next to them; not only does it feel like it, but you can see the bed move and the depression of where someone is sat can be seen. Better than that, in my opinion, is the strength of this ghost; it moves the beds before and when people are in them. The best I have heard is three people sat on a bed and it moved a few inches.

Accompanying the beds moving is the shaking and rattling floor. I know this sounds like an earthquake is happening in the rooms, but this does not happen in any other room; it is all localised to this room. The floor seems to vibrate in some way and you can feel it in your feet as it happens.

The Curtain Twitcher

There are various strange noises that occur in this room. One of them may be caused by bats, as there is a colony of bats around the castle and sometimes they can be heard scratching away above you. If you want to see them the best place to stand is in the courtyard, outside the refectory, as you get the light from the building illuminating them as they sweep around the grounds.

One strange noise that you do get in here is the same noise you can hear in the state apartments. It seems we have a ghost that likes the sunlight as you can hear the curtains being opened in this room as well. Of course, when you turn around and look, the curtains are still closed.

The Constable's Room

The chaplain's room does not get a huge amount of activity but when it does it is spectacular. I have already mentioned the sound of footsteps above you when the room is empty, and I have talked about the sound of children playing on the stairs outside the room. So now I can tell you of a very interesting BOL that appears in here.

The BOL

The Ball of Light that appears in this room is a whitish one and not too bright, but the interesting thing about this one is that it tends to follow the same path each time. It appears around the middle of the floor and heads towards the fire exit at about floor height, and then disappears.

One ghost hunting guest thought that it actually was a ball on the floor illuminated by their torch and bent down to try and pick it up; as she did so the BOL disappeared.

Flapping Doors

We have had reports of flapping doors from this room, with the door opening and closing of its own accord. We have told groups that it may be down to a breeze as the door does move on windy days. We were then informed that it did not just open, it swung open at full force, so perhaps our door opening ghost gets around the castle and not just in the refectory.

As well as a moving door, perhaps our bed hopping ghost comes into this room occasionally, as we have had reports of a vibrating bed. It shakes when no one is touching it or even moving anywhere near it. I think the castle should cash in on this, charge extra and claim it has a massaging mattress.

Physical Personal Attacks

That makes it sound much scarier than it is; a personal physical attack does not necessarily mean the image that it conjures in your mind. Do not worry, it is highly unlikely that a spirit will drag you kicking and screaming from your pub and glue you to the ceiling whilst it indulges in a spate of heavy tickling. What that term means is anything that physically affects you has no normal means of explanation.

There have been people fainting in this room, people being sick, the sensation of choking, and being strangled. Strange smells can emanate in this room from nice ones to hideous ones; some that stop as soon as you walk out of the room. I don't mean the kind of smells that the occasional ghost hunter, having eaten too many sprouts that day, may make; I mean really rancid, putrid, offensive smells that hang around for about five seconds and then completely disappear, and other times sweet smells like flowers.

All being sceptical ghost hunters, my group dismissed these symptoms, putting it all down to mass hysteria, and three of them went in there one by one; all fell foul of exactly the same effects.

We are well aware that if you take a group of people into an environment where they are expecting to be spooked, then it is possible that mass hysteria will occur and a room full of people will suddenly all feel sick and faint. Yet the smells are a lot harder to discount as it is a physical event witnessed by many people, all giving the same description.

The Oubliette

This room was possibly used as a dungeon and possibly has a working oubliette in it. Under the floors of this room is a large empty cavernous hole that may have been used as a dungeon. At least in the prison in the west tower you may have been released, or executed. In here you were just forgotten about and left to starve to death.

Oubliette comes from the French word to forget. When I give tours of the castle all anyone seems to comment on is the fact that they know what an oubliette is because there is one in the excellent Jim Henson film called *Labyrinth* (which if you have not seen I can heartily recommend).

If you were lucky, you died by landing on your head and the fall killed you; if you were unlucky, you lived. Sometimes, you were thought of as entertainment for the gentry folk of the castle, who would come along and poke fun at you as you lay in a pit of your own waste. There are reports of cannibalism in the oubliette pits as it may have been your only source of food.

So, after that description I hope you have a decent night's sleep, and do not sleep in...

The Oubliette room window, looking out onto a particularly cold day.

The Scary Bed

A large amount of phenomena is associated with one bed in particular in this room, and if you want an interesting night then I guess this is the bed to stay in. The events do not happen very often; we get several reports a year from guests who are staying and know nothing about the ghost stories.

The people who get scared and leave the castle half way through the night have often slept in this bed. We have tales of cyclists who stayed in this room, booked for a few days and left in the middle of the night never to return; we have had groups of ghost hunters booked to stay the night in this room that have left screaming and crying in the middle of the night. One woman was so disturbed that she was found the next day, sat in the King John's Lounge crying, and refusing to go back into the room to even pack her bags.

So the big question is why? What happens in this bed that is so scary? One of the answers is the ghost that wants your duvet. There have been many, many reports of people waking up in the night because the duvet has been wrenched off the bed. Obviously, lots of children probably put this down to other kids in the room messing around, but it gets really scary when you are the only person in that room.

One guest was not that perturbed by the whole situation though, the next day staff went into the room and noticed that he had moved the bed, firmly up against the wall. They asked him why he had done this, and he sad that it was the only way that he could keep the sheets on the bed as all night something was pulling them off of him. I can honestly say he is a braver man than I am.

Another reason why you may be scared is the screaming. Many people have reported the sound of a woman screaming whilst they have been lying in this bed; we have reports from tourists, children, teachers, ghost hunters, foreign students, people from all walks of life and from all over the country or even the world that have reported this without knowing the story beforehand.

The sound of the children can also be heard in this room from the floors above and in the corridors; we have had tales of people complaining, about the groups of children in the constable's, and the chaplain's room, only to be told that there are no children staying in the castle.

Temperatures Going Wild

I know this title sounds like it should be at the start of a Jerry Springer show, or Jeremy Kyle should be saying it to you from his smug demonic face whilst introducing some sex crazed housewife with two hundred lovers. Sorry, this is not that story, instead it is about thermometers. Not so exciting I know, but probably more interesting if you are a ghost hunter.

Very often when a place is haunted you will get sudden temperature fluctuations, because ghosts can make a room go very hot, or all of a sudden go very cold. The extreme examples of this can be seen in the oubliette, we have had multiple thermometers in a room all showing vastly different temperatures.

During one experiment we did, we placed three thermometers about two foot apart from each other, and at one point one of the thermometers read seven degrees Celsius and the one that was four foot from it showed 21 degrees Celsius and the middle one showed 14 degrees Celsius, so at least this ghost could do its seven times tables in degrees for us. These temperatures would fluctuate massively and quickly, with it going up or down every few seconds. This continued for a good ten or fifteen minutes and then suddenly stopped. We have experienced this, and so have many other ghost hunters many times over the years.

BOLS

Yet again we have our Balls of Light appearing; this time they tend to be of a white or blue nature, and tend to come out of the trap door that leads into the oubliette. These can be seen with the naked eye as well as night vision cameras.

The Touchy Feely Ghostie

You may think you have chosen wisely by convincing your friends that they can have the scary bed. You think you may be in for a nice easy relaxing night of listening to your friend scream his head off as the duvet is ripped from him.

BUT BE CAREFUL, you may be in the not so scary bed; as you walk through the door, the bed on your left has had many an incident of people being touched up in it. Now, that sounds a lot more interesting than it actually is. Do not expect any hot ghost action here. People who sleep in this bed report the feeling of being stroked by an invisible arm; a few of our ghost hunting group have experienced it, and not found it too pleasant.

Bruce was sleeping in this bed one night and I was in another bed; not the scary one though, I'm not that brave. We were both woken up by something falling onto the floor; we both woke with a start, and I shouted: "Excuse me Bruce my good man, would you mind telling me if you know what that disturbance was?" I'd like to think I said that, but the actual sentence contained a lot more expletives and me saying, "What was that?" We calmed down very soon as we realised it was Bruce's phone that had fallen on the floor, and jut as we were both closing our eyes again and heading back to sleepy land, we both sat up and said, "Why did that phone fall on the floor?" There was no reason for it to have moved, and as it was early in the morning, we decided to get up early and have breakfast instead of staying in the room.

Conversations

The first time that Phantomfest ever came to the castle, it was in the middle of the day, and they were filming for a documentary. Paul and I walked around the castle to get some interesting shots and went straight to the oubliette room.

From the other side of the door they heard people talking as though there were at least two people in the oubliette room. They decided to go upstairs and film there instead. Returning downstairs they noticed the conversation had stopped, and the door was locked.

On checking they found out that no one had been in the room at all and that the door had been locked all day. To be precise the keys had not even moved from their cupboard all day, so no one could have even accidentally left it open for people to get into.

Rattling Chains and Padlocks

I do like it when ghosts fall into character properly; they should wail and moan and rattle chains. Well, this one does to some extent; it rattles the padlock on the oubliette gate.

Now some people may say that could be the effect of people walking on the floor, somehow making it move and sound like it is moving, while others say it is the building cooling down at night and causing the metal to contract causing a minute movement in the structure of the padlock which then makes it move.

These would all be plausible explanations if it was not for the fact that the padlock moves quite violently, and not just moves once; it can rattle away for a few seconds sometimes. People have even seen the thing look like it is being lifted up.

One word of warning about the oubliette is that if you are fortunate to be able to see down it, do not let anything fall down there. Once it is in there it stays there as there is no means of getting it out. One Hallowe'en a skeleton was placed down there and he has lived there ever since. We did manage to retrieve a mobile phone that was dropped down there using a great deal of fishing equipment. If you look down into the oubliette you will see Bob the skeleton and between his knees there is a large glass pendulum; this was accidentally dropped when a group of ghost hunters were pendulum dowsing over the trap door when I walked in quite loud and quickly. This startled the person holding the pendulum and she screamed and dropped it, and that was about three years ago. So hold onto your phones and wallets if you lean over the trap door.

Mary

Many people have used Ouija boards in the castle, many mediums have visited, and there have been many séances, but one name that occurs again and again is Mary. Unfortunately this is such a common name and I am sure in the castle's history there has been someone living here called Mary.

The story gets slightly better when the details are filled in though, as most people tend to give her an age of around fourteen; they say she worked at the castle and did not live here.

Perhaps she is the source of the female screams heard in this room.

Recordings

We have some excellent recordings taken in this room that have managed to capture the sounds that are often reported; unfortunately not the screaming or the children, but the sound of footsteps and furniture moving. We often leave sound equipment recording in locked off rooms, especially in a building this size, as we do not have the time or number of people to investigate everywhere.

What we captured in here is truly amazing; it is the sound of someone walking around on the wooden floor with heavy shoes, and the sound of furniture like a chair or stool being moved across the floor. The best thing about the recording is that all this happens just before Emma walks into the room and turns off the digital recorder; we hear her open the door and walk in, at no point does she acknowledge anyone there, and we know for a fact that the room was empty and everyone was accounted for.

The Black Shadow

The Black Shadow strikes again, as he is seen near the fireplace in this room; whether he is the same black shadow we do not know, perhaps the castle is inhabited by the Black Shadow family, as they do seem to get around a lot. One thing about this castle is that it has changed shape a lot over the years on the inside, with walls and staircases being rebuilt or demolished, so what may have been one room in the past is now four rooms. Therefore it is not hard to see if a ghost is haunting an old room how it may be seen in several rooms.

When people do their paranormal vigils in the castle they tend to have low lighting or the lights off, believing that if a figure is a very faint image then the light can interfere with it and then it will fail to materialise.

When the lights are off in the rooms, you can then see under the doors if someone walks past the room holding a torch. This light is often seen, or feet are seen walking along the corridor or down the steps when no one else is in the castle.

Groups in this room have heard people moving around on the stairs and walking about, and yet we have had cameras, and witnesses, to prove that there was nobody there.

THE WEST TOWER

The Hanging Room and The Guard Room

The Figure in the Doorway

Many people have witnessed a dark figure; yet again, we see a member of the Black Shadow family appearing, although this one seems to have more of a human form than the others do. So much so, that sometimes its features can be made out and distinguished. Some people have seen just his legs standing there, and others have seen what looked like a silhouette stood in the doorway; even though they don't see his features they say it feels like he is looking at them.

I was sat in the hanging room doing a ghost hunting vigil, and I heard a strange noise like someone talking about two foot to my left, at the same time Vix was with us, a hardened sceptic. Vix said she saw a strange shadow moving towards the door area, about two feet to my left.

Floating Lights, BOLS, and Mists

There are reports of strange green lights that are square or rectangular in shape, and can be seen floating around in the hanging room. I have seen it myself whilst sat in one of the window alcoves on a ghost hunting vigil with a novice ghost hunter. She was sat next to me holding a night vision camera trying to work out how to use it and staring at the screen. I then saw this green rectangular shape about the size of a can of red bull float towards her.

I was rather dumbstruck and could not say anything. I just watched as it got closer and closer to us, and eventually touched the other ghost hunter on the shoulder. She

View of the West Tower The Hanging Room at the top, with its tiny slit windows, similar windows in the Prison on the first floor, and the Porter's Lodge at the bottom.

turned to me and said, "What did you do that for?" At this point I regained the power of speech and said I that did not do anything, and what was she talking about.

"You just grabbed my shoulder." I pointed out to her that my hands were in front of me and that there was no possible way that I could have grabbed her. I then explained what I saw, and watched as she got up and left quite quickly. I did not watch for long as I was hard on her heels not wishing to be alone in the room.

These are not the only lights seen in the hanging room, there are BOLS seen mostly next to the doorway above the bed, while various flashing lights and colours float around for seconds at a time. There is also a mist that seems to float above this bed both in the hanging room, and also the bed next to the doorway in the guard room.

The Tap on the Window

The group of ghost hunters known as PARASOC was spending an evening in the castle the night before a Phantomfest ghost hunt. Several members were sat in the hanging room on various beds and boxes, and also sat in the window alcoves. A loud noise came from one of the boxes that they were sat near to; this was followed by a tapping noise

The window in the top left corner is the guard room leading into the Hanging Room.

on the window. If you have been in this room you know that there is nothing on the other sides of the windows, there are no trees, and it is a very tall building so unless someone can levitate they are unlikely to be outside the windows.

The way it was described to me was that it sounded like someone knocking on the glass to get your attention, as though they were outside on the lawn trying to get in. Only two floors up John, Dave, and CJ, all members of PARASOC, said at exactly the same time:

"What was that?"

The investigators all swapped seats, and the tapping was heard again, meaning that if for some reason one of them wanted to fake the noises, they would not be able to. They had changed places and yet it had happened a second time; they changed places again, and this time they heard a knocking on a wooden box in the room.

They were impressed by this display, and became even more impressed when they asked it to repeat its actions; however it did not. Instead the group was treated to a massive banging noise, as though something had hit the middle of the floor in the room, so hard that they even felt the vibrations through the floorboards.

As you can see from this window on the floor below we are already at tree level. There is no way anyone could tap on these windows without using a dangerously tall ladder.

Foreign Witnesses

The best witnesses in my opinion are the ones who have nothing to gain and did not have any ulterior motive. So, on that basis, when we get stories from our foreign guests I find them much more interesting as it is unlikely that these people will have spoken to anyone in this country about ghost hunting. My favourite story is from a Canadian man who was staying in the hanging room and awoke to see a woman in period costume walk across the room and kneel down in the corner of the room. He told the staff first thing in the morning, and looked rather pale when he did.

This guest was not as shaken as the young Spanish student who also saw the same thing about a month later. A group of young students were staying in the room and apparently this one young guy awoke to see the same image, and the description he gave was the same as the Canadian man had given.

I cannot think why a young Spanish student would have met up with a Canadian guy to come up with some strange ghost story, to do nothing other than try and scare some members of staff at a foreign castle. Not only that but the Spanish student would have had to be a great actor as apparently he was inconsolable, and in tears over the whole affair.

Marbles

In the guard room, a noise like the sound of marbles falling onto the floor is heard. It does not matter how many times you hear the marble noise there is never anything on the floor to find. This noise has been heard on several occasions by many witnesses, sometimes simultaneously which means it is unlikely to be an auditory hallucination.

Footsteps

There is no surprise to know that we hear footsteps in the hanging room, but we will come on to that in a moment; first I want to tell you about our ghost that walks up the stairs.

From the landing outside the Prison up to the guard room there is a lovely solid wood staircase. Wooden staircases obviously creak and move when the building heats up and cools down, and often noises like these can be mistaken as footsteps. Thankfully, through years of investigations, we know the difference, as the ear becomes accustomed to what all these little noises sound like. We have often heard the footsteps come up the stairs. Bruce described that he had a group in the guard room and they heard someone walk up the stairs so he opened the door to let them in, but there was no one stood there.

The most prevalent haunting in the castle has to be the footsteps and movement in the hanging room though. I have often been in the guard room and heard people moving around in the hanging room, and when you walk in there the place is empty. One of the best examples of this is when you are in the Prison, as this room is directly below the hanging room. I have been sat in the Prison on my own, with nobody else in the castle at all; I have locked the place up and I have the keys in my hand knowing there cannot be anyone but me here. Whilst lying in my bed in the Prison I could hear someone walking around upstairs and then what sounded like one of the stools get dragged across the floor. So, being a brave ghost hunter, what did I do?

I put my headphones on and watched a film on my laptop, too scared to go up and check that it was not a burglar; oh, what courageous ghost hunters we are.

Grabbing Ghosts

We have another touchy feely ghost in this room; this one is not a stroker, or a strangler. The ghost in the hanging room tends to grab people on the shoulder. This happens in the hanging room and occasionally in the guard room. In the guard room the spirit tends to brush over you when you are in bed, and people report the sensation of being stroked by something like a soft blanket. The best reports of these are from people who have slept in the room on their own as obviously it could not have been anyone else moving blankets around. We have had a few of these reports including one from a ghost hunter in my own PARASOC group, whom I trust completely.

Messy Spirits

If you are working at the castle I guess the ghosts can be most unwelcome guests; we forget, because we are ghost hunters that not everyone likes the spirits who wander around when you are just trying to get on with earning and honest pound or two.

One of the previous castle managers tells a fantastic tale of one annoying (annoying for him that is, great for us) poltergeist incident. He was cleaning up in the hanging room, and had just made all the beds up. Back then the YHA policy was that they made all the beds up, unlike now, where the guest just takes duvets when the bed is slept in, which environmentally is much better leading to much less washing needing to be done. The whole room was perfect; he then decided he would do the beds in the other tower, back then the fire alarm was a different system and he turned it off from within the room so that he could open the fire exit and walk across the bridge to the east tower. PLEASE DO NOT DO THIS, there is a different fire alarm in the castle now and if you open the door it will set it off, and you will have to explain to the fire service why they have been called out when there is no fire.

Anyway, back to the story: he walked across the bridge, did the room in the east tower and then walked back across; when he arrived back in the room, all the duvets had been thrown onto the floor and pillows were scattered around the room. Personally, I think it is a great excuse especially if you have not done any work and your boss turns up:

"Why is the place such a mess?"

"Sorry, it was the poltergeist."

EMF results

Whilst filming orbs, the paranormal science group PARASOC from Cheltenham, managed to film them flying over EMF meters (Electro Magnetic Frequency). As the small white orbs flew over the EMF meter it went off and registered some form of disturbance, which is rare. Most of the time EMF meters will go off for various reasons but to see something like an orb set off one of these things is like gold dust to a ghost hunter.

The Bedhopper Strikes Again

Well, our friendly bed hopping ghost from the chaplain's room may have walked across into this tower, as one of the beds in the hanging room had several people sat on it and moved several inches. It is possible that the chaplain's room and the hanging room were one room at some point throughout the years so it is possibly the same ghost in what was the same room.

The Heavy Breather

I find noisy ghosts far more disturbing than visual ghosts, partly because if you can see the ghost you know where you should avoid. If a ghost is stood on one side of the room I know I can stand on the other, but when it is just a noise and the 'spirit' is invisible then you are in trouble as it could sneak up on you at any point. In this room I think I would get slightly scared on my own if I was lying in bed and heard the heavy breathing ghost that has been heard in here. Not only does it breathe heavily, it also murmurs and whispers, so you could get scared and paranoid that the ghosts are talking about you at the same time.

Scrying

There is a practice used mostly by trance mediums called Scrying, a technique I teach whilst doing the Phantomfest evenings. I always say when doing any of these experiments that we show people what to do, but that does not mean that we believe in them, instead we take a totally neutral stance on the practice, and if it works then we look at the possible reasons behind it. This is one experiment that seems to work on ninety percent of the people that do it, and is a very strange and unnerving experience.

Guests sit in front of the large mirror in the guard room, and stare at themselves in low light, the idea being that you are allowing your own body to be taken over by whatever spirits are in the room. This will show itself by reforming the features on your face into someone else. Often you will look at your image and see various features change shape, or the most common being that the face will disappear and another face will return in its place. This face will often start talking at you, and you can see its lips move when you know that your lips are not moving at all.

Whilst doing this experiment we seem to always get an image of a woman who looks like she has had a stroke as the right hand side of her face seems to have been affected. The first time this 'face' came through we had a psychic artist by the name of Stephen Cox, (www.stephencoxart.com) giving a demonstration at the other end of the castle and he seemed to draw this face at exactly the same time as we were seeing it in the guard room.

The sceptic in me says that in a dark room, staring at yourself in the mirror, your eyes are bound to play tricks on you, and all you are seeing are things that anyone would see in low light. This is most likely true, but what is amazing is the amount of recurring stories and events when we do this in the guard room. Very often, people sat at the mirror will say they can see a figure stood in the doorway behind them. I have been stood with a group and asked what they could see, and the man doing the scrying said that he saw nothing except for the six people stood behind him, at which point I counted and there were only five of us.

Another thing that often happens when we are sat there is that we are all in the guard room, and we can hear something move around in the hanging room, when we look through the door we can see that there is no one in there. There are other strange things that have happened during this experiment, such as guests being pushed. We heard noises in the empty hanging room; one guest went to look, as she got to the doorway she came flying backwards and whilst she was lying on the floor she claimed that something had pushed her. Another guest was sat scrying and thankfully I was not far from her as she came flying off the stool and I caught her before she hit the floor; she said exactly the same thing – something had grabbed her and tried to throw her to the floor.

I am not saying whether I believe in scrying or not, but it is an interesting experiment to try for yourselves as I have tried it and it is fascinating. One word of warning though; like Ouija boards, this practice can become quite addictive, so do not do it for too long otherwise the lines between reality and non-reality become slightly blurred. We do not want you being carted off in a white coat to somewhere padded, with your arms tied behind your back.

Get Off My Chair

This pushy ghost may be the one that is responsible for pushing people in the hanging room; the layout of the rooms changes from time to time but for a long while there was a box on the left in the window alcove as you walk into the hanging room on your left.

People have been sat on this box, or near it, and report that they have been grabbed or pushed, as though something does not want them there.

Very Funny

When we have been in the hanging room, we have heard laughter coming from beneath our feet in the prison; however, we know at the time there was nobody in there. This has happened the other way around as well; when in the prison, laughter in the hanging room is heard, so perhaps we have some mice in the floorboards that do very good impressions of human laughter; either that or we have a ghost that likes to see us running up and down the stairs a lot. Maybe it's the ghost of a former P.E. teacher trying to get us to do some cardio vascular exercise.

The Prison and the Room Outside

One thing to note whilst in the prison is the amount of graffiti on the walls. Please do not add any of your own, as some of this graffiti is hundreds of years old, including a curse that can be found carved into the walls of one of the window alcoves.

Misty Figures

This time we have a misty figure, as opposed to our family of black shadows that roam around the castle; this time, it is seen in the first alcove on the left as you walk into the Prison.

Another Grabbing Ghost

The castle is full of touchy feely ghosts, or perhaps just one that gets around the building a lot. Many people get grabbed whilst in the prison, and clothing can be pulled from time to time. As I am writing this book, I am looking through my notes and I see the last time this happened was about a month ago, when two non-ghost hunting guests were staying (a father and his teenage son) and in the morning they reported to the staff that the teenager had been grabbed on the arm and the dad had been grabbed by the hand.

I have experienced the hand grabbing myself. I was stood with my back to the wall on the left hand side of the cell as you come in, and something held my hand. There was no mistaking it; it was as if a small hand had hold of me and was moving my arm, it felt weird but not disturbing or scary. We have also been stood in that room watching one of the PARASOC ghost hunter's coats moving as though being pulled by something, which we all found fascinating. I think the guy wearing the coat found it slightly more disturbing than we did.

This ghost tends to touch people on the arm, and the most likely place that you are going to experience this is near the main door into the cell, or between the doorway and the first window alcove. It normally grabs you by the right hand, arm or shoulder. If you do stay in the castle and any of these things happen to you, please get in touch and tell us, as we try to keep a record of everything that happens in the castle. You can also tell the staff in the morning and they will try and write down everything that you can remember in their ongoing ghost book.

The Growling Ghost

The dark Shadow strikes again. Near the fire exit we have seen a dark figure, and more disturbingly this figure has been heard to growl on occasion. The growling noise can be heard in here without the figure appearing as well. The best thing about this happening is that more than one person can hear it at the same time, which is always more impressive and believable.

Bruce was in the prison once with a group of ghost hunters and saw a figure stood against the wall, behind a bed, near the fire exit. This was one of those vigils where all the lights were off yet there was a small amount of light coming through the windows. The figure eventually disappeared and Bruce realised that no one was there; when they turned the lights on they also realised that there was not enough room for anyone to be stood where Bruce had seen them, as there was a radiator between the bed and the wall so there was no room to stand.

A Ghostly Breeze

The problem we have is that this is a draughty old castle that is over 800 years old, so controlling the temperature is difficult. However, even on a still evening the temperature will suddenly plummet as a cold breeze seems to walk around the room.

BOLS

Of course we have our famous Balls of Light, but this time they are normally of a blue or white colour. Some of the most spectacular footage I have seen involving BOLS comes from this room, with one performing the most amazing manoeuvers and then flying straight towards the camera at great speed, causing the cameraman to duck as though he was about to be struck by something.

Knock Knock, Who's There?

Paul and I were called to the Old Kitchen to witness some poltergeist activity; unfortunately, by the time we got there, it had died down to nothing, so instead we walked up the stairs and were about to sit on the landing and window seat at the top of the old kitchen staircase. As we reached the top we heard something small land on the floor. It sounded small and light like a small stone; we could not find it, but as we turned to look, Paul saw the prison door moving and shaking of its own accord. At the time there was nobody in the prison and if someone had just opened it we would have seen them. Unfortunately, I did not see the door move as Paul was stood in front of me, but I did hear the movement. Other groups have reported this noise since.

The best instance of the door rattling came from an investigation one evening; as I was in the guard room, another group was in the prison, another in the old kitchen, and another in the state apartments and corridor. I heard the prison door rattling, so I came down the stairs to be confronted with the group coming out of the prison, and another group walking in from the corridor. The prison group asked me if I had been rattling the door, and I replied that I was about to ask them the same thing. The group in the corridor had come in as they had heard people outside the prison and came to see who they were. We all then went downstairs to the old kitchen to ask if anyone down there had done it, but they insisted that they had all been sat quietly and not moving for the last twenty minutes. I would have had to doubt one of these groups had it not been that each group had a member of PARASOC or Phantomfest with them who confirmed what was being said.

Footsteps

As usual we get the footsteps again, whilst in the prison we have on many an occasion heard people and furniture move around upstairs in the hanging room when there is no one up there. We rushed out of the prison and up the stairs to see absolutely no one there, and nothing but an empty room.

Sometimes we have rushed up there, still heard people in the hanging room, and when you walk into that room through the guard room, you are confronted with an empty room and silence. Even when there is nobody but us in the castle we have heard furniture, footsteps, and sometimes voices, yet we know it cannot be anything human as we are all in the one room together.

The Old Kitchen

One feature of the Old Kitchen is the strange looking wheel above the window facing out into the gate house tunnel. It is a 'Dog Spit' which is a small tread wheel that a dog would be placed in, and as he walked along the wheel would turn the meat that was on a spit over the fire. This is one of the only original wheels *in situ* in the country.

Tom the Poltergeist

Now we come onto one of most popular ghosts in the castle; he is a young boy who goes by the name of Tom. He is a poltergeist who does not like men but likes women. How we came about all this knowledge I will tell you.

Tom's best appearances are in the form of a poltergeist, as he tends to throw stones around. Actually, 'throwing' stones is probably the wrong word to use, as the stones are dropped out of thin air rather than thrown. When you throw something it follows a path called a ballistic curve, and anyone who can remember their science lessons will know that if an object is thrown it curves with the curve dropping off rapidly as the item's energy is lost and gravity takes over. Well, these stones just fall in a straight line straight from the ceiling. If you are in the castle, look up and you will see the castle is a sealed unit, and plastered, so anything falling from it would seem impossible.

View taken from one of the haunted staircases looking down into the Old Kitchen.

These stones drop from nowhere, and land in the middle of the room, which has been witnessed by several groups throughout the night with up to twenty people at once. During one of the Phantomfest evenings, three different groups sat in the room and saw stones fall from the ceiling. On these evenings the groups just write down what has happened and do not tell anyone until they all meet up at the end of the night, so none of the three groups had breathed a word of this to each other, and they were very shocked when the others started telling the same story.

When it was revealed that this had happened, thirty people sat in there and saw it happen again. They tried a Ouija board, as these groups often do. We do not condone or condemn this practice but allow groups to make up their own minds as to their accuracy. One woman said that the stone throwing was impressive, but that if whatever was there could throw stones, then it should throw one at her; before she finished the sentence, a stone bounced off her shoulder.

Another night everyone had been told about the stones and one woman didn't believe it; she went straight to the old kitchen after we had all swapped our stories and experiences. She sat down on the small sofa at the bottom of the stairs and said out loud that she thought everyone was mad and that none of this stone throwing had actually happened, at which point a small stone landed on the sofa next to her.

"Fair enough" she said, got up and walked out.

The Dog Spit, a small dog would be placed in the wheel and as he ran it would turn the meat on the fire.

One film crew was filming when a small stone fell directly in front of them, falling right in front of the lens. PARASOC members have been in the castle and seen stones fall in front of them when no one else was in the room. Bruce was conducting experiments, trying to replicate the trajectory of the stones by throwing them against the walls, and bouncing them off the ceiling; time after time he failed. He was about to give up and turned around to tell us that he could not do it and a stone dropped right in front of his eyes.

Why do we call him Tom? Because we have been visited by hundreds of ghost hunters through the years, including sceptical ghost hunters, believers, and mediums, and a lot of the time they will come up with the name Tom associated with this room; and that he is a boy, aged somewhere between seven and ten. As I said, I do not claim that any information gleaned from Ouija boards, séances, and mediums has any relevance whatsoever, but before the total sceptics dismiss it out of hand you must remember that we have been doing this ongoing investigation for years now, and we have seen a statistical anomaly towards this name and age. We are not talking one in every twenty people calling, giving this description and name; instead it tends to be about one in three. This story, as far as I know, has not appeared on the internet, and we do trawl the internet checking on regular occasions. The groups that give these descriptions are very often not connected with each other in any way and are unlikely to have colluded to deceive us.

People have felt like they have been grabbed by unseen hands whilst sat in this window area. It is normally women that are affected, and it tends to avoid men.

The reports that the mediums give, and that séances tend to throw out, tell of a young boy who was mistreated and does not like men, or men that look a bit like me, with broad shoulders and big build, and somewhere between five foot ten to six foot. This seems to be borne out in the fact that there may be amazing activity going on in this room, and as soon as I, or people that look slightly similar, step through the door, it stops. He does, however, trust women, and the only times that he is seen are by women.

One of whom was a previous manager of the castle. She was saying goodbye to a school party, and as they drove off slowly down the narrow road, she went running after them. The reason for her Olympic sprinting bid was because she had seen a young boy in the old kitchen through the window, and thought the school must have left someone behind. She got onto the coach and they did a head count and proved that everyone was there; she then did another Olympic run back to the castle, thinking that someone was wandering around in there. Thankfully, there were other staff in the castle and they could verify that no one had come in, and when they searched the castle no child could be found.

A Fidgeting Ghost

I have taken many of my friends to the castle, in a vain attempt to get them interested in my hobby. One of my friends thinks I am insane for sitting around in dark damp buildings in silence for hours on end. Thankfully, she understood slightly why I do these things when she was sat in the Old Kitchen with one of our ghost hunters, listening to something moving around on one of the leather sofas opposite her. She claimed that it sounded like someone sitting down and moving around trying to get comfortable, and had gone on for several minutes, but it stopped as soon as I came in to find her.

The Ghostly Hand

A partial apparition has been seen on the staircase a few times, walking down into the old kitchen. Not a full bodied manifestation, but just a feminine- looking arm and a hand, which in my opinion is probably even scarier.

More People Than There Should Be

You have to remember that a lot of the time these ghost hunters like sitting in the dark; it is very rarely completely black in a room as they may have a dim torch on or the light from the fire exits is shining, along with the heaters giving off a fake warming glow from the little lights inside them.

One room which never gets completely dark is the Old Kitchen; groups will sit in there for ages chatting away, and on a few occasions you get up to turn the light on and someone in the group makes a rather shocked noise. When asked why, it is because what they thought was a figure sat by the table turns out to not be there. One guest said she knew someone had been sat there as she could see the outline of someone against the lights coming from the electric fire. She had not commented on the fact as she had assumed it was a real person in the room, albeit a rather quiet one.

Not Really A Ghost

My favourite story is from one of the cleaners and is not really a ghost story at all. She came down the stairs one day, and got the fright of her life, because at the bottom of the stairs, sat on one of the chairs, was a woman in some form of period costume, which was most definitely not of this century or the last. She moved closer towards the spectre, until eventually she touched it on the shoulder. To her surprise, the figure screamed and spun around to look at her; this spectre got an even bigger shock when the cleaner also screamed. It turned out that unbeknownst to the cleaner, a group of historical re-enactors were staying in the castle, one of whom was sat with her headphones from her ipod in, so had not heard the cleaner creep up on her.

Porter's Lodge

Not a huge amount of activity goes on in this room, so if you want a trouble-free sleep this is the one to head for; although it does mean walking through a room with a poltergeist in it every time you want to go to the toilet.

The Always Opening Doors

Staff from Phantomfest often stay in this room, partly because we can get a decent night's sleep without fear of being woken up by ghosts, but also because it is the closest to the car park and we bring in lots of equipment. It is because of all this ghost hunting equipment that we keep the doors closed at all times. On several occasions we have returned to the room, we would find the doors and fire exits open. I would like to stress that the reason this seems odd, is that the fire exit is bolted from the inside so you cannot open the fire exit from the outside, and also this is before any guests arrive so the only people going in and out of that room are the Phantomfest team.

Whilst sat in the room I have experienced the opening doors, as I have heard the outer door into the old kitchen open, which is followed by the door of the porters lodge opening, as though someone has just walked in. This also happens the other way around, when the door of the room opens quickly, followed by the door into the old kitchen opening, this time as if someone has just walked out.

Hagging

There is a story from one man about how he woke up and felt that he was being pinned to the bed and could not move. I include this story as it is probably a very good example of hagging, or the naturally occurring phenomena that leads to the incubus and succubus stories of old.

There is state of consciousness just as you are falling asleep, and just as you are waking up, where your body is swapping from one state to the other. Anyone who has shared a bed will know this when their partner is drifting off into a deep sleep and occasionally will talk complete gibberish. You ask them a question like, "Have you put the bins out?"

If the reply you get is something about a giraffe trying to catch a balloon, you know that a dream world has somehow been entered. This state of semi-consciousness is called either a hypnogogic, or a hypnopompic state. Quite often, when in this state, the body becomes paralysed, which is a very good thing because without it we would all act out our dreams; there have been cases of people being killed because someone was acting out a dream, and their partner was in a dream world in which a zombie from Mars was trying to suck out killer's brains. The best case of this was a man in America, who, in his sleep, drove to his wife's parents' house, murdered them both and then drove away again and was found naked asleep in a field.

Thankfully we have not had any Martian zombies or naked murderers roaming the castle; this is down to sleep paralysis. The problem with sleep paralysis is that when you are paralysed you are dreaming, and in the half-awake state your mind can think it is awake when in reality it is not. This leads to a nightmare happening even though you think you are awake.

Due to the fact that the body is paralysed and now panicking it starts to think: what is it that is holding me down like this? At this point, it often invents something sinister and makes you dream or hallucinate an entity that is responsible for your lack of movement. In medieval times, when man invented many things to do with their image of God and the Devil, you would naturally think it is a demon, and due to sexual suppression this would often lead to the thoughts of being raped by a demon or Satan. Thankfully, we live in a world that seems to have shaken off a lot of superstitious religious belief, and so we are more likely to associate this with something like a burglar, or an attack from a real person; it is all about frames of reference. So, if you believe that you are staying in a haunted castle, or even if in some subconscious way you associate castles with ghosts, the likelihood is that you will dream up a ghost that is holding you down.

I have experienced this form of hypnogogic state and I must confirm that it is absolutely terrifying. Thankfully, I had already studied the subject and so my brain managed to grasp reality and realise what was happening, at which point it ceased and I could move again, as I 'woke up' for a second time; only this time I was fully awake.

More Rolling Coins

I was lying in bed on Saturday morning after a hectic night of ghost hunting; in fact, the day before had been Hallowe'en. Paul was lying in a bed on the other side of the room, and we had Vix with us, a reluctant sceptical ghost hunter. Above us, we heard what sounded like a coin rolling along the floorboards. We thought we had better check if there was anyone up there, as hopefully we could have gained a spooky pound or two.

When Paul ran up there he met a group of confused ghost hunters who insisted that a coin had just rolled along the floor from nowhere, straight towards them.

The Crying Baby

As is often the case, the night before a Phantomfest ghost hunt I will stay at the castle, so that I can be there in the morning to set up the event, but it also means that I am often sharing the castle with other normal everyday paying youth hostel guests. We try not to make it obvious who we are if there are children around as we do not want to frighten them, but in the morning when we start putting on our Phantomfest T-shirts people always start asking questions about ghosts. We normally give in and take everyone on a ghost tour of the castle, telling them the main stories.

When I told one family of the crying ghost, the father jokingly said that they must have heard that when they were in the Porter's lodge, as all night the sound of a baby crying could be heard coming from the room above (the Prison). He then turned to another dad that was with one of his kids, who had stayed in the Prison; he said to him:

"But I guess that must have been your baby; perhaps it was being troubled by the ghosts in the Prison".

"We don't have a baby. I thought it must have been from your room."

"We don't have a baby either."

Suddenly, the expression of jokiness faded, and the two dads turned a slightly pale colour as they fell silent once again.

THE GROUNDS

Gate House, The Grounds, and The Car Park

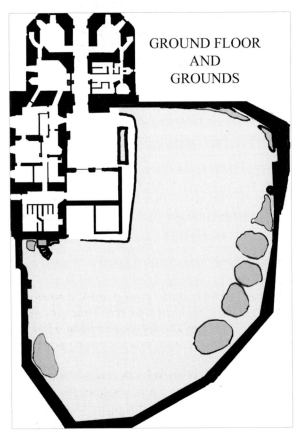

GROUND FLOOR
AND
GROUNDS

Even when the castle is closed to the public you can still go ghost hunting here, in the grounds and car park. These areas on their own have more ghosts than many other haunted castles put together.

The stocks, next to the fireplace, in the old castle wall.

The Knight

If you have been on the internet you will know of the knight in shining armour that is seen in the grounds; sorry to disappoint you, but he has not been seen for a while, certainly not in the years that I have been here anyway. What has been seen, however, in the daytime and at night, are misty figure near the fireplace where he is reportedly known to walk.

Knock Knock, Who's There? Part Two

A polite ghost who wants to come into the castle does not just walk through the door; he knocks first. If you go to the castle you will see two very large, and more importantly, very heavy doors. We have been stood next to the doors late at night and heard knocking, as if it was someone wanting to come back in after getting something from their car. We have opened the doors and there is no one there.

The sceptical reader may think we are in a village that has kids who are probably bored and they are having a game of cherry knocking just to annoy us. If you know the castle at all it is impossible to be at the door, knock on it, and then be out of sight in less than five or six seconds. There is a long, cobbled pathway with walls either side that used to be the

The very heavy castle doors, with the YHA logo on the front.

drawbridge. We have tried replicating the knocking and then running away and no one, not even the fittest and youngest, could get away without being seen.

One member of staff let someone in late one night after hearing the knocking, and as the person passed them they felt there was something not quite right about the new guest, and so turning around to confront them, they noticed he had disappeared completely.

This story has also happened in the middle of the day, with previous staff letting people through the gates, and as they turn around to talk to them they have already disappeared. One thing to note here is that in our experience, if you can see a ghost, do not take your eyes off them, as if you turn way when you look back they are often gone. Ghosts can disappear before your eyes, or fade into a mist and then vanish, but more often than not, it is when you turn your head to tell someone to come and take a look that it will go, almost as if you have moved the antennae on top of your TV and lost the picture.

If you are at the castle you will notice the size and weight of these doors. I have already told you a story about the refectory, where the doors and latches open of their own accord. The night after this happened, we were stood in the gatehouse tunnel area and telling the guests about this happening; one of the sceptical guests kept coming up

The tunnel through the Gatehouse where many horses have been heard trotting along, and many footsteps have been heard walking.

with possible theories as an explanation. We have been ghost hunting for years now and had obviously thought of all the explanations that we could come up with and tried and tested these ideas to prove they were not true. He still did not believe us, and almost as though exasperated by the whole situation one of the ghosts helped us out. The doors flew open at such speed and ferocity that they banged hard against the castle walls; suffice it to say, our sceptical observer did not offer any more explanations.

Feel free to try and move these doors and you will see it takes a great deal of force, and is therefore highly unlikely to be something as simple as a draught coming through the main entrance tunnel. We tried to replicate the effect and continuously failed, even with Paul and me running at the door; with full force, throwing them open, we could not get the same effect.

Footsteps

Once more, we have our ghostly wanderers; footsteps are heard by people sat in the rooms off the main entrance tunnel, which tend to walk from the gate to the main castle. A lot of the time these ghostly feet go unreported due to the fact that people assume there is someone walking outside. It is only the people in the Old Kitchen who tend to report this as they have a window that looks out and they can see there is no one there. We have had groups reporting people being noisy when they have had vigils going on in the oubliette and the Porter's Lodge (the fire exits of these rooms lead to the main gate), and we have to tell them that there was no one outside their rooms.

These groups have not only heard footsteps and chatter, but also the sound of horses walking past the fire exits and along the main entrance tunnel and into the courtyard.

Something In The Trees

We always tell our ghost hunters that you are just as likely to see a ghost outside in the grounds as you are in the castle; you have to remember that there are just as many parts to the castle that have fallen down as there are still standing. So, if a ghost haunted the old court room, or the Keep, then they would to be outside now, not inside.

Telling ghost hunters this and getting them to investigate, however, are two different things. Often we come here in the castles' off season so in the middle of winter it is very cold and wet, so it is hard to get volunteers to wander around the muddy, soggy gardens and moat. When they do, they are rewarded with strange sightings. A hooded figure is

The trees growing where there once was castle wall and a Norman castle keep.

seen, and every time it is, we have to check it to make sure it is not some teenager from the village climbing the walls whilst wearing a hooded top. Most of the time, I must tell you, it is not an annoying teenager; it defies explanation. Sometimes there is often something seen behind the trees moving around, and often ghost hunters are too scared to look, especially if they know about the big cats and wild boar in the forest. When they do look, whatever was there disappears.

The Floating Legs

As you walk into the castle through the main gate, take the time to look up above you, as a set of legs and feet have been seen wandering around on what would have been the floor levels of the destroyed sections of the gatehouse.

Disappearing People

One guest saw a figure walk out, from what he later learned, was the fake door. This is the doorway on the opposite side to the Old Kitchen. This figure walked around the corner towards the grounds; the guest thought it was actually one of his friends and ran

Not such much legless as bodiless. The legs were seen floating as the floor collapsed many years ago.

The door that leads to nowhere, this is just for show and does not open, yet this was the door that someone walked out of just before they disappeared. For the Orb spotters amongst you notice the two orbs in shot. Reflections or Spirit lights, you decide.

after him, but when he reached the corner he realised there was no one there, and that the door does not open as it is a fake door.

More Falling Stones

A large stone, approx 6 inches by 4 inches, rolled towards a few people stood near the doors. It moved fast, as though it had been thrown. Another group, sat on the bench at the refectory end of the gatehouse, heard the stone and saw that it could not have been thrown by anyone. If it had fallen from the upper floors then it would have bounced, but this seemed to travel as though rolling along the floor, as if a ghostly bowling team were playing skittles with our ghost hunters stood near the door.

Undead Parking Attendants

One area that often ends up populated by guests is the entrance to the castle, partly because you are not allowed to smoke in the building. Another reason why outside becomes popular is because when people get really scared they often go out to the car

What was once a moat on one side of the entrance is an ornate pond, and on the other side it is now a car park.

park and try and sleep in their cars. In my opinion, this is ill advised, as the car park seems to have an attendant of its own; a member of the dark shadow family. I have seen what looked like a silhouette of a figure walking between and through the cars, and this has been witnessed by several of our ghost hunting team. It also seems strange that people who are scared want to sleep in their cars; because they are now staring out of their windows looking at a graveyard.

One thing I want to point out again is: remember that these stories have happened again, and again. I could fill up the book with stories that have only happened once, but we try and ignore them until another person can come along and confirm the tale. I urge every reader of this book, if you are serious about wanting to see a ghost, then go and spend the night at the castle. At the time of writing it is possible to have bed and breakfast there from as little as twenty pounds a night. If you want to go on a night when the castle is open purely to a ghost hunting night then go with a reputable ghost hunting group and don't pay more than about thirty or forty pounds for the night. One thing I must insist on, is that if you see anything, or hear anything, then please tell the castle staff, and the Phantomfest group (www.phantomfest.co.uk)

A WORD OF WARNING

Some people think that looking for ghosts is a big NO-NO, that we are dabbling in affairs that we know nothing of, that we are tearing the thin divide between the land of the living and the evil of the after world, that we will all become possessed by demons and devils, and the world will be taken over by flesh eating zombies. What I can say is that there has never been a case where people have been attacked by demons and ghosts; although there are those who believed that they could be attacked by them, from countries and social environments that believe in this sort of myth, people who do feel as though it happens; in countries where these myths have died off, or did not exist in the first place then it does not happen. Most psychiatrists believe that there is a type of placebo effect, that people get affected in some way because they want to be, or expect to be.

Saying all this I have seen people get injured and affected, but most injuries happen as someone is running out of a haunted room screaming and then they fall down the stairs, or run straight into a book shelf.

There are, however, a few people in the Forest who do not believe we should be doing this, one of whom is the vicar at Lydbrook church. In a newspaper article in 2009, he spoke out against ghost hunting, psychic evenings, mediums, Ouija boards, and so on; yet, after reading the article, this may be due to the fact that a sheep's head dripping with blood was found on a pole outside his church. This was immediately put down to devil worshippers causing havoc and mayhem. The fact that it may have actually been kids, or trouble-makers thinking this would be funny, and may well have had nothing to do with ghosts, Satanism, or anything other-worldly at all.

From past experience dealing with newspapers, I am sure that the extreme viewpoints that you come across in articles written about such anti-parapsychology petitioners are full of misquotes, and things taken out of context. I have been in many a newspaper where they have not even been able to spell my name correctly or print the correct age, and when simple facts such as these are misreported then what hope do we have with something as sensational as religion, and the supernatural.

So, in my experience, it is important to keep a level head; if something looks too scary do not get involved, if people ask for vast sums of money do not get involved, if there are people who say they can answer all the questions you have then walk away; they are full of what at best could be described as delusions, and at worst falsehoods and lies.

So should you now wish to continue down the path of the parapsychologist then here are a few more words to help you on your way.

CHAPTER 6

MORE INFORMATION ON HOW TO BE A GHOSTHUNTER

In my previous book, *Paranormal Cheltenham*, I gave you a brief outline of what things to do and use in a paranormal investigation. Hopefully, you have read more about the subject and wish to even visit the venues that I have written about. So consider this lesson two on our master class on being a ghost hunter.

Scrying

I talked earlier about Scrying when I mentioned the large mirror in the Guard Room of St. Briavel's Castle; well, I will tell you a bit more about it, and how to do it.

The idea behind it is actually an ancient one, as Egyptians used to use it to try and communicate between priests throughout the country; it was a psychic internet connection, or a telepathic telephone. Back in Egyptian times the priest would fill a black bowl with water and stare at it for ages and then eventually tell everyone that Bob's auntie had just had a baby, or that someone else could supply their psychic telephone at a much cheaper rate if they swapped scrying providers.

Today, it can be done using bowls of water, and it is a similar method to that employed by the gypsy fortune teller staring into a crystal ball. Most people, however, use a large mirror instead of the antiquarian ideas; for some reason, people think that using a mirror is more plausible and has less black magic mumbo jumbo attached to it. What I can say is, try it; it is an interesting experiment. The trance medium will tell you it is a way of communicating with the subconscious, in the same way that we have talked of Ouija boards in previous books. The sceptic will tell you that it's a trick of the light after staring at a low light reflection for hours on end.

So, how do we do this? Try to get some very low lighting in a room; the way to do this is to take a torch and cover it with pieces of paper until you have managed to obscure the beam enough to still be able to see, but the beam is diffused enough so that there is no direct light shining into your eyes, or the mirror. You will need a mirror that is big enough to see your whole face in it, and some of the background as well. Sometimes, when doing this experiment, the background can change so as big a mirror as possible is needed.

Now sit in front of the mirror, relax and stare at yourself; the best way to look at yourself is to somehow feel as though you are looking through the mirror, not at it. Your eyes will start adjusting, and the trance medium would then try to invite whatever is in the room to take over his face and show himself. The image in the mirror, after a while, will start to transform into someone else's face, or you will see yourself but with slightly different features. If you are lucky, the mouth on the reflection will start to move, and talk to you, or you may start talking and speaking in a different accent or style that you are used to.

As soon as you want to stop, the mediums would say close your eyes for a few seconds, turn away from the mirror, and ask whatever it is to leave you alone. I hasten to add that I tell you how to do these things, but it does not mean that I necessarily believe in any of these experiments. All that being said I have done this one, many times, and whether you believe it or not it is a very entertaining, and interesting, experiment.

Psychometry

Psychometry is a fascinating experiment that is totally cost free, which as a ghost hunter is a phrase I love; we pay out anything from one hundred to a thousand pounds on night vision cameras, and video units, even going up to one and a half thousand pounds for a reasonable thermal imaging camera, so anything free is great.

It is all about the art of reading an object and getting facts about a person, place, or event from holding an item. This is a great experiment to try when you have nothing else to do and you are stuck in a ghost hunt at four o'clock in the morning, quietly sat waiting for dawn to arrive. (Why she is always late I do not know.) When dawn does finally break you get up and then drive, after three cans of red bull, and arrive exhausted at home at six o'clock in the morning. So try psychometry; it's simple.

Choose someone in your group, ideally someone that does not necessarily know too many of you there, or does not know much about you. Give them an object that you carry around a lot; a wallet, a ring, car keys, etc. Failing this, try handing them an object that has some extreme form of significance, maybe some heirloom handed down from father to son since the dawn of time. This person, then without any hint whatsoever from you, has to say out loud any pictures, images, emotions, thoughts, or just words that spring into their mind. Remember, you cannot be wrong in this experiment, as it is all about what is coming into your mind. Repeat this experiment with everyone having a go with different objects, and after a while you are likely to find someone in your group who is very good at this.

The way to easily and quickly check the 'science' aspect of this is to write down their reading of the object and compare it to another object supplied by someone else. Take the first reading and score it for accuracy; if the reading was transferred to a second object, or if the first reading is just as accurate for another object from another person then the first reading must have been so generic that it counted for nothing.

You will be amazed at some of the results from this; the trick is to say everything that you think of, so do not try to censor yourself in any way. What may seem ridiculous to you, may be spot on for them. You may say something stupid such as, "I see a troll living in a house, with a white picket fence." Of course this would be ridiculous, until you find out the person who supplied the object lives in a house called 'troll view' and has a white picket fence.

Calling Out

Many groups use a technique called 'calling out'. This is used to ask direct questions or pose some form of direct provocation to the spirit or entity. This normally happens after sitting in a quiet dark room for half an hour and realising that it is going to get very boring doing this for six hours. So you need to ask questions such as the classic, "Is there anybody there?" to which someone in your group will probably do the joke, "Knock once for yes, or TWICE for NO!"

Another one is, "If you are here then perform some form of physical phenomena, such as appearing as a light form, or touching one of us." This again leads to some smart ghost buster piping up with the phrase, "Don't touch me though".

It may be a good idea to think these questions through before starting; you may be in a haunted castle and already know some of the history, so it could be a way of testing the spirits' knowledge, or whether someone is playing a trick on you. It may be that you know nothing of the history and whatever questions you ask could be slanted so that the spirit gives you evidence that you can later check. Be prepared though, because if you are not then you will all be stood in a dark room all thinking of very vacuous and boring questions.

Weather Watching

Weather can be a very important factor of ghost busting. Some people believe that to experience a haunting the weather has to be the same as when the murder, suicide, slaughter, or accident happened. The event somehow becomes recorded in the fabric of the environment and by replaying the conditions as best as possible then the image will also replay.

It seems that the stereotypical ghost story or horror movie featuring a thunder storm may not be over-dramatic. Some reports claim that water is very conducive to haunting, so it is possible that we will see more ghosts during a thunder storm. The sceptic will also say that during a thunderstorm we revert to more primeval emotion and the fear reflex kicks in, and that it is this that makes us scared, as well as a type of placebo effect makes us see the ghosts.

So in your reports try and note the temperature, the time of day, the humidity, rainfall, light levels, etc. Then on subsequent investigations at that place you may find a pattern emerging.

Example of Report Forms

Report forms can vary wildly, and my groups produce reports varying from one page through to two hundred page epics. The very basics need to include the date, time, and location; these are obviously extremely important. More important is anonymity; you may have a case with sensitive information in your reports, and places that do not wish to be in the public eye, so always get permission to publish these facts.

You will also ideally record the weather conditions, temperature, EMF fluctuations, and humidity levels throughout the evening.

Then write up a personal account of what happened, from as many ghost hunters who went on the investigation, as people's personal experiences of the same phenomena can differ wildly. Then include the myths and legends of the story and the reasons you went there in the first place. With any luck, your personal experiences will match that of the myths surrounding the haunting. If your personal reports vary, they are just as important as the original stories from the location, as other groups may go along and experience exactly the same events as you did.

Zenner Experiments

The zenner experiment and variations of it is the most famous psychic test ever created. It even features in one of the greatest movies ever made, *Ghostbusters*; alright, that is debatable, but I do not think you will find a true ghost hunter that has not watched the film. In the film, Bill Murray is trying to get people to guess which shape he is holding up; they are printed on cards and consist of five different shapes. The typical ones are: Star, Circle, Square, Triangle, and Wavy Lines. There are many variations on these images and feel free to use which ever shapes, words, colours, etc that you want.

One of you sits looking at the card and the other person sits, ideally, somewhere where they cannot see the person who is staring at the cards. The first person looks at a random image and tries to think only of that image, whilst the second person attempts to tune in psychically and guess the card's image. The more times you can repeat this experiment the better, as it is a great tool for proving statistically whether someone is psychic. If you have five images and sixty times out of one hundred you guess correctly, then this is a statistical anomaly and should be looked into as it may be evidence of telepathic powers. If you guessed correctly no more than twenty out of one hundred then this is no more than mere guess work and you will not be appearing in the next series of *Heroes*.

Photography Orb Problems

Some of you will have, by now, visited Clearwell caves, The Fountain Inn, or even stayed the night in St. Briavel's castle. You may be very excited, and have shown off to all your friends the pictures of spirit lights and orbs, that people get so worked up about on programmes like TV's *Most Haunted*. Well, yes, your photos may show the first manifestations of a spirit taking shape, but it is more likely that it shows a collection of dust near the lens. You may be very excited because in one picture they are there and in the next photo taken a split second later they are not. I am afraid a lot of this is to do with focal length of lenses and aperture speeds. I do not wish to condemn all orb photos as mere dust as there are some remarkable unexplainable light anomalies caught on tape and film, but most are dust particles.

The best way to judge it is if you saw the orb with the naked eye. If this happened and you managed to get a photo this is much more evidential. If you have managed to get to your camera in time (let alone managed to not run screaming out of the room), then try and point to the orbs in the shot so it is obvious to someone looking at the photo that you could see them.

I have seen entire books dedicated to spirit photography, and after having read them, they have said nothing about focal length and light refraction on dust. However, there are excellent scientific papers on this, and even the camera companies themselves will tell you of these problems.

Computer Software

You do not need expensive equipment and software for this hobby. If you have a laptop then this will be amazing for analysing results. There are excellent resources that are freely available online. A lot of people use 'Audacity' which can be freely downloaded to analyse wave forms and audio recordings. Now, do not blame me if you download computer viruses trying to get free software; you may have a laptop like mine with Windows Vista that seems more haunted with things that go wrong than most of the haunted locations I have ever been to.

I do not wish to publicise software and hardware too heavily as it makes it sound as if I have a cut in their profits, but a good audio analysis tool and a photo viewer or editor are key tools that prove very useful.

Imaging software needs to be able to zoom in to pixel sizes, with the ability to cut, crop, and alter colour balances and lighting wherever possible. There are quite

well known software houses out there that offer a lot of free downloads from their home pages, so you do not need to spend hundreds of pounds on the latest version of Photoshop.

Film editing software is also very useful; if you manage to get great footage, you want the world to see it. Most laptops will come with a Windows movie maker built in, but there are great cheap alternatives. I use Ulead to edit my videos but there are countless alternatives. Make sure you save your footage at the highest resolution you can; there is no point putting out a piece of film, saying look at this strange light anomaly, if it is all so pixelated that you can't even see people's heads properly.

When posting films onto the internet there are sites like You Tube, Metacafe, etc, but do be aware of the wishes of the person who owns the property that you were filming in. If it is a private house they may not wish to be inundated with ghost hunters, or worse still, reporters. Also be aware that these sites often allow people to leave feedback, which will more often than not, be offensive to you in some way; they may call you a Nutter! Or that you should get a life, or that you faked the film. Do not in any way be offended by these idiots, you know what you saw and experienced, and that is what matters.

The true ghost hunting community is always interested in other group's results regardless of what ethos the group has; their beliefs will obviously give a flavour to their results but good ghost hunters can see through this and look at the evidence presented. On a personal level feel free to email evidence to my ghost hunting group as we are always interested in other groups reports, photos, and videos.

CONCLUSIONS AND FURTHER READING

Further Excellent Books to Read on the Subject

In the process of reading this book, many newspaper articles were read, internet sites trawled, and witnesses spoken to. I easily have enough stories for another two books just in the Forest of Dean. Hopefully these will see the light of day, but I always want more so if you have any interesting stories or 'haunting' to tell me about please feel free to contact me on the PARASOC website or through www.phantomfest.co.uk. Until that time then I recommend reading through some of these titles.

Andrews, Ross, *Paranormal Cheltenham*
Addicot, Ian, *Haunted Pubs of the South West*
Bryant Duncan Dena, *Ghost Stories of the Forest of Dean*
Cameron, Janet, *Paranormal Brighton and Hove*
Cinderey, Lyn, *Paranormal Gloucester*
Guttridge, Roger, *Paranormal Dorset*
Law Sue, *Forest Ghosts*
Meredith, Bob, *Cheltenham a Town of Shadows*
Meredith, Bob, *The Haunted Cotswolds*
O'Dell, Damien, *Paranormal Bedfordshire: True Ghost Stories,*
    Paranormal Hertfordshire
Poulton, Smith, Anthony, *Paranormal Cotswolds*
Ritson, Darren, *In Search of Ghosts: Real Hauntings From Around Britain,*
    Paranormal North East
Scanlon, David, *Paranormal Hampshire*

Felix, Richard, *Ghosts of Gloucestershire DVD*

Go to www.parasoc.org to read investigation papers and report any more Forest of Dean ghosts. If you want to go ghost hunting and are too scared to just head out and try it alone, then look at Phantomfest's website and see if they are doing any nights at St. Briavel's castle.

You may even end up featuring in my next book — who knows?

Locking up the castle after a scary night of Spook Spotting.

*See you all in the next book with many more
true stories to scare you to sleep!*

Also available from Amberley Publishing

Paranormal Cheltenham
Ross Andrews
ISBN: 978-1-84868-630-4
Price: £12.99

Available from all good bookshops, or order direct
from our website www.amberleybooks.com

Also available from Amberley Publishing

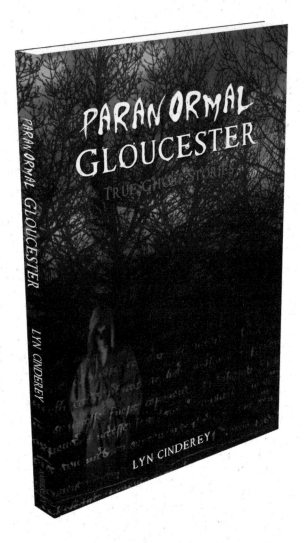

Paranormal Gloucester
Lyn Cinderey
ISBN: 978-1-84868-249-8
Price: £12.99

Available from all good bookshops, or order direct
from our website www.amberleybooks.com